THE ART OF DECISION MAKING

HOW TO MAKE EFFECTIVE DECISIONS UNDER PRESSURE

TIM CASTLE

K
N
O
W
N

www.get-known.co.uk

I dedicate this book to the memory of
my loving, inspiring,
and remarkable mother, Anne Castle

"You're donating the time of your existence to the things that you give your attention to, make sure that what's taking your energy is worth your life."
Idil Ahmed

CONTENTS

PART 1

MY STORY

INTRODUCTION

WHAT DO YOU do when you realise you are only seconds from imminent death? You make an effective decision. A decision that will save your life.

Somewhere inside of me, deep within, it was already written, but the decisions that I made and the actions that followed as a result on that fateful day quite literally changed the course of my life forever.

Although I really learnt about decision-making in a moment of crisis, making sharper, quicker decisions has become a way of life for me now.

This has made me more effective across all my endeavours, and now I want to teach you because mastering the art of decision-making is one of the most critical skills you can learn to take ownership of your life, improve your leadership skills and advance your career.

Decision-making is one of the most highly sought after skills when companies select candidates to promote into positions of greater responsibility. On top of this, effective decision-making improves your confidence, self-belief, and you'll naturally experience more success across all areas of your life.

Learning how to make good and quick decisions is not just going to improve your overall quality of life, it's something you do for you, your family and your personal aspirations, to see what you are really capable of and how far you can really take your goals, dreams and ambitions.

My improved decision-making has not only had a gigantic effect on the results I have been able to achieve but also the speed at which I can work. In the pages that follow, I'll share with you the vital decision-making lessons that I have learnt during one of the most life-changing experiences I have ever had, and I'll show you how to apply them in everyday living. But before I do, I want to ask you this question.

Why are people who make quick decisions more successful?

One of the key reasons is that people who make a decision and then action it are more likely to garner feedback from the world. They quickly reach a point where lessons can be learned, allowing them to pivot, finesse and tweak. If you think about a start-up, the quicker a founder can get a minimum viable product out into the hands of the target audience, the quicker they can gather feedback and adapt their product to meet the needs of the people they are trying to serve. This is where value is created. Whether you are running a start-up or not, quick decision-making creates a cycle of progression through the key stages of evaluation, action, re-evaluation and improved action. This is the secret weapon that propels you forward.

Decision-making and taking action is an art that comes from balancing the need to move forward with being cautious. It means timing the opportune moment to take action and strike, to maintain your resilience to carry on when times get tough and the energy starts to drain, as well as seeing the bigger picture and still focusing on the tiniest of details. The art of decision-making is all-encompassing and requires your full attention, as your body, mind and soul are all connected to moving through the decision and living it out in a state of flow.

What I mean by this is that effective decision-making doesn't just come from picking an option with haste, somewhat randomly. Instead, it requires careful, balanced thought, based upon the information available at the time. Decision-making is a muscle that you can build, and in this book, I'm going to show you how...

When you take consistent and committed action to follow through whilst focusing your whole being on the job at hand, you will beat procrastination to a pulp.

CHAPTER 1

OFF TO A FLYING START

IT WAS LATE autumn on a wet and foggy day as I sat perched on top of the Aga in the kitchen (for those unfamiliar with an Aga, it is an old-school storage stove and cooker made out of heavy cast iron with two heated lids on top, which heats the whole house). I was nestled in my favourite spot, the familiar dip in the left lid, which had been carefully sculpted from 19 years of consistent bottom-warming. My parents were good to me, damn good!

Maybe it was because she felt sorry for me (I had dropped out of a joint honours Chemistry and Psychology degree at Birmingham University a month earlier and was now working shifts at Tesco as a non-food stock controller). Trust me, there are only so many Britney Spears CDs and copies of *The Office* DVDs you can look at before it gets boring. Maybe it was because she knew this would light me up inside, or maybe it was just an opportunity too incredible to pass up for the both of us.

She read her physiotherapy magazine with excitement. and said, 'Six days, five nights, in Verbier, Switzerland, studying physio and skiing in Europe's premier alpine destination. How fantastic!' she exclaimed, a plan clearly formulating. 'Can you imagine… I really should do this, and I'll see if you can join me. What an opportunity!'

She had found an advertisement for a skiing and physiotherapy lecture holiday taking place in the snow-capped mountains of Verbier, Switzerland. It sounded epic, like something out of a movie! The fact that Mum was even discussing this was promising because when she got an idea in her head, there was no stopping her. I could tell from her voice there was a combination of determination and pronounced possibility.

Within the space of a few hours, my mum – true to form – had lovingly convinced my dad that this was a perfect idea, made a few phone calls to inquire about availability and got the OK to bring her teenage son along for the adventure as well.

This was typical Mum – pushing to overcome boundaries and hurdles, and only seeing possibility. This was Mum in her true spirit. Once my mum had an idea, her boundless enthusiasm took over, and she brought it to fruition. It was one of her best qualities. Mum made all the arrangements and enlisted the help of my ever-passionate, creative Auntie Judy, who is always full of 'make it happen' gusto. She wouldn't be joining us, but she's someone who's where the fun is at. If there's something wonderful happening in the family, she is there, helping, doing whatever she can to make it even better.

Auntie Judy was drafted in to source extra accommodation for one night prior to the start of the chalet stay with the rest of the physiotherapists on the ski trip. When Mum and Auntie Judy planned a trip, it was like a flame lighting the fireworks. They were both highly excitable, positive, love-the-fun-of-it kind of people. If there had ever been any doubts about this trip happening, they were quickly snuffed out once the two of them had got together on the planning committee. I knew it was ON! I was going skiing in Verbier!

Once Mum and Auntie Judy discovered that a hostel in Verbier had once been an underground bomb shelter, well, there was no stopping them. I was destined to spend a night underground in a World War Two piece of history.

At 19, a snowboarding trip to Switzerland was a dream come true. I would have stayed in a garbage can if it meant I could be near the fresh powder and mountains. As a huge X-Games fan and a snowboarding fanatic, this was my idea of heaven.

The idea of ski trips represented everything that was awesome about life to me; physical exercise in the day and copious amounts of partying and socialising in the night. My only prior experience of skiing had been as a child in Abernethy, Scotland. We would go every few years and pray for snow. If we got lucky and there was enough real snow, we could get off the dry ski slope and into the mountains for real (I can only recall this happening on a handful of occasions). In Scotland, conditions were often poor, icy and cold, with little to no visibility, so skiing back then was more about experiencing the log fires and heated swimming pool, the hotel games night and spending time as a family on holiday.

Scotland aside, my only other experience of skiing was on a school trip to California. We spent a few days at Heavenly in Lake Tahoe and I got to try snowboarding, which opened my eyes further to what winter sports were all about. OK, I'll admit it, most of my knowledge up to this point had come from watching endless reruns of the *Winter X-Games* in my living room at 5am before school and playing video games like *Cool Boarders 3* with my mates (now I am really showing my age). Now you can see that this trip was like winning the lottery for me. It was a dream come true at the exact time that I needed pushing towards a new focus.

***

A couple of weeks later, at 4am, we hit the road. My dad and sister drove Mum and I up to Leeds Bradford Airport to send us on our way. Back then, trips like this weren't a regular occurrence. It was kind of a big deal and the significance of it didn't escape me.

We didn't travel internationally an awful lot as a family, so this was a special occasion and one that I was determined to make sure I squeezed every drop of gorgeous alpine satisfaction from. Bring on that plane! Our spirits were high and the thrill of what was waiting for us on the other side was immense.

I knew this trip was the start of something big, just taking it was inspiring, and I could feel my mind beginning to expand. A few weeks earlier, I had been sitting alone and rather depressed in the bowels of Birmingham University, drifting in and out of consciousness while listening to lectures on protons and electrons and the chemical composition of... I don't care. I was thinking: *Is this it? Is this my life for the next three years?* Everything I had worked so hard for had brought me to this point and I was not a happy chappy.

Truth be told, I had signed up to this hybrid course with the goal of switching to Psychology later and ditching the sciences. What I hadn't counted on was that every Psychology student with straight As had also decided that Psychology was the best thing since the birth of the M&Ms McFlurry and were therefore not wanting to give up their place for me. I had reasoned that after a couple of weeks, spots would start to open up and I could glide into place and pursue my goal of studying the subject I was most passionate about without a hitch. I had taken a chance, but it hadn't paid off. I had moved my life to Birmingham only to find out that life didn't want me there.

On top of this major glitch in my plan, the accommodations office had messed up my application for housing and for some strange, unknown reason I was assigned to join the mature students' wing. This meant that whilst everyone else was off making fun friends for life with people their own age, I was chatting to John, a 37-year-old from Manchester, about the state of the economy and wondering why I had been so bothered about going to university in the first place.

At the airport, for the first time in a long time, I felt a zing of excitement about my life. I was waiting to board a plane to paradise, which would take me on a trip aligned with my purpose. Not only did it tick all the boxes as an extreme adventure holiday, it also filled me with a sense of fulfilment. I WAS DOING SOMETHING I WANTED. This trip mattered and it planted the seed inside me that would begin my love of adventure and travel, as well as my desire to take the bull by the horns and go for it.

> **This attitudinal change in my approach meant I began to believe in myself. I now knew when I was doing the right thing for me, rather than doing what other people wanted me to. It was my first big step to taking control of my life, and that was really exciting.**

I hadn't exactly quit Tesco's yet, but mentally I was well on the way. The cogs had begun turning and the memory of work faded discreetly into the distance like a sunset disappearing below the horizon. You are aware of it and then all of a sudden, it's gone.

As we made it on to the plane and took our seats, I felt like I was about to burst. This was the life I wanted, one of exploration, possibility and freedom. Once we got up in the air, I remember clearly looking out the window and wanting this to be my life, then realising that it was, and telling myself that I had to do whatever it took to achieve this jet-set lifestyle. This was when I discovered there was a certain glamour to flying; something about being picked up and transported from one place to a whole new world left me feeling whole, grateful and delighted that we had made the decision to take the trip. Now you've got to remember that this was probably only my third ever international flight. I was over the moon; I had permanent rose-tinted glasses glued to my face. There were most likely little kids screaming in the seats behind me and grumpy passengers moaning about the early start, but I didn't see any of it. I just saw endless fluffy white clouds, radiant blue skies and a world of possibility that had a heartbeat called freedom.

It was an amazing feeling to be taking a trip, just Mum and me, into the unknown and to go for it with no holds barred. I loved the spontaneity and enthusiasm for life that Mum had. She just went for it. If there was a mission or an idea that she believed in, she owned it. And thanks to her, I was on the trip of a lifetime.

When we touched down in Geneva, the sun was shining, and beautiful royal blue skies took over for as far as I could see. We had left behind a cold and miserable grey morning in England and replaced it with this fresh, crisp, gorgeous Swiss picture-perfect scene. It was like an advert for Toblerone.

After we located our driver at arrivals and began the 4-hour drive to Verbier through the valleys, the excitement really started to kick in. Here we were, travelling through the Swiss Alps. There were eagles soaring high up above, people on the radio that I didn't understand and the most phenomenal landscape that my extreme-sports-mad mind could endure.

A couple of hours went by and we reached the foot of a precarious-looking winding track that snaked up the side of a huge mountain face. The terrain started to change. Up until this point the journey had been relatively flat, but this was something new, not what you would get in England and certainly not to be attempted at the speed we were travelling.

Our driver was obviously a dab hand at manoeuvring this lumbering minivan around the 180-degree hairpin bends with skilful grace, having done this trip multiple times a day. For me though, it was a harrowing experience as I sat in the back, peering out to look over the edge. As I did, I couldn't help but imagine the van careering off the side.

> When faced with new, unknown experiences, our minds play tricks on us by focusing on the worst-case scenario, such as the driver losing control and driving off the edge, and then us being trapped in the minivan as it rolled all the way down the steep incline as we faced a painful and violent death.

Looking back, this is a simple example of how quickly what we focus on and our perspective can take over our reality. It was a good job I wasn't driving, as thoughts such as these could have quite literally been the end of us. But we were in the safe hands of Enrique, who looked as calm as a sleeping baby as he deftly drove us up the mountain face.

After 45 minutes of snaking back and forth, with my heart in my mouth for the entire uphill climb, we pulled up to the centre of Verbier town. We had finally made it and I was blown away; it was like nothing I had seen before. The villas and log cabins looked like something out of a movie – perfect snow-capped rooftops in a majestic winter wonderland. I don't know what I imagined but Verbier was better, way better.

Admittedly, I hadn't done much research on Verbier; being a teenager, I didn't have time for it. As long as I had my headphones, MP3 player and punk rock music, I was set to go anywhere.

I soon discovered that Verbier was a very glamorous ski resort. It was the kind of place the exclusive set came to party, ski and let their hair down. Like many of the famous European ski resorts, it had an air of sophistication about it, a winter wonderland nestled in the heart of the Swiss Alps. If I thought that the drive from the airport looked like an ad, this was on steroids. I half-expected Mariah Carey to jump out singing, *'All I want for Christmas is You.'* This was the most of everything I had ever seen – the most luxury, the most snow, the most fun I had ever seen.

Verbier had beautiful women, alcohol and exclusive nightclubs. I later found out that it was a favourite destination of Sir Richard Branson who owned a chalet there, which thrilled me no end. I was among the rich and famous in a billionaire's playground, and although I knew nothing about this world before arriving, I was enthralled. For me, it was about the music, the cute girls in snowboard gear and making friends. I could not wait to get stuck in.

After trudging around the snow-banked roads of this wondrous town for some time, we located the WW2 underground atomic bomb shelter. It was, as you'd expect, hidden from view. It looked like a regular chalet except for a small sign that read 'The Bunker', which gave it away. We checked in and found our room. It was authentic alright, a cement heavy no-frills box with little done to dress up the fact that this was, in fact, used during the war to protect civilians from the wrath of an atomic explosion. During the

Cold War, Switzerland went on an atomic bomb shelter building frenzy and built enough to house the entire Swiss population with space left over.

As we made our way around the premises there was a sombre feeling to it, but all the same, we were both in high spirits, too high to care that we were 50 feet underground surrounded by metres of thick cement and a rather damp, chilly atmosphere. It was seriously like something from a James Bond film. There was no daylight and no windows. This hostel is not recommended for guests with claustrophobia.

To add to the authenticity of the hostel experience, Auntie Judy had another surprise up her sleeve. We weren't in a private room – oh no, that wouldn't have been the true hostel experience. Instead, the dorm had rows of triple-stacked bunkbeds. As it turned out, we were sharing the large dorm room with just two cool-looking Swedish dudes, Sven and Boris, who had long, blond flowing hair down to their waists. It was odd, marginally uncool, but given how bizarre it felt to be staying in 'The Bunker' to begin with, this detail went largely unnoticed.

After our little foray into Cold War Switzerland, we dumped our belongings, and off we went to get kitted out with ski gear.

Then we headed up to the slopes for a quick, late-afternoon ski. The adrenaline was now pumping; we had finally made it to the main event. My mum was on skis and I was on a snowboard. As we had only ever been skiing in the highlands of Scotland together, it was a truly special experience to venture onto the continent and discover new territories. There was a real sense of adventure between us.

As we glided cautiously off the chairlift and began to ease our way down the first slope, we both found a natural rhythm, as muscle memory kicked into gear and elation overcame me. This was living! We managed to squeeze in one run before deciding we had sufficiently broken in our ski legs (I think the early start to the day was beginning to catch up with us) and a nice cold alpine beer was on the agenda instead.

As we walked into one of the many lively bars at the bottom of the slope, I felt at home. The vibe was young, hip and friendly, the kind of bar where everyone looked super cool and super chill.

In all honesty, I freakin' wanted to be them! Any of them! I wanted their lives. These snowboarders looked so effortlessly cool, living the good life up here in the mountains. There is something so rewarding about being in the outdoors and with people who are having fun. There's an energy and a youthful joyful outlook on life. It was electric and I wanted to be them. I felt like I was finally in a place where people understood what I was all about, with people who had a similar outlook on life and I could relate to.

I had always known deep down that I wanted to work a ski season, but hadn't done anything about this, and the positions had been filled with these spectacularly cool guys. If only I could have been one of them, instead of working in Tesco.

Note: this was a fixed mindset to a problem. What was actually holding me back was fear, disguised by my perception of what was possible. Instead of listening to my true self, I told myself that it was OK, I could cope at home. I told myself I was too late, that I had missed the boat rather than face the fact that I wasn't sure how to pull off getting a ski season gig. What if it didn't work? What if I didn't like it? My dream would be shattered and who wants to live with a shattered dream. Better to tell myself that it was too late and save any potential mishap. I rationalised that it was better to stay at home in my house fantasising about working a potential ski season, rather than take any action. After all, university had been a disaster. I'd never actually considered making it happen, but now that I was facing the reality of how awesome it would actually be to work a ski season, my mindset had changed. I started to figure out ways to make it possible. A surge of FOMO overtook my fears and I connected with a deep passion inside of me. I knew that working a ski season was something worth fighting for. In this state of exuberance, I started to believe that such a life could be available to me and the bud of an idea started to poke its head out of the soil and grow.

It was also cool being there with my mum. She was cool with the vibe and could hold her own with any of them. I didn't feel embarrassed, just proud. Mum also knew when to leave me to it and give me my independence by taking her cue to go back to the bunker to get ready for dinner. That gave me the space to sink another beer with the mega-cool bartender and let my imagination run wild as I thought about what it would be like to live this carefree lifestyle with only snow and parties to worry about.

As *Californication* by the Red Hot Chili Peppers played out across the hum of a packed mountain resort bar, I couldn't think of anything better than being right there, right then.

My sense of adventure was piqued, and I beamed from ear to ear. I couldn't believe that I had only left a dreary cold Leeds Bradford Airport this morning and now, ten hours later, I was sitting in this bar surrounded by all of my favourite things. Life really is miraculous, when we say 'yes' and are open to the possibility of change.

Looking back, I didn't really know how to put a plan into action as a teenager. What I have learnt in the years since, and what my experiences have taught me, is how to put a strategy into action that gives me the maximum opportunity to go after an idea and bring it to life. Back then, I was letting fear do some of the talking rather than love and faith, and I definitely wasn't following my gut. I also didn't understand that mindset and emotional state is an important driver of decision-making and that when I felt called to do a ski season in Verbier, it would have been the perfect time to start asking questions about jobs and using my excitement to overcome any fears.

That evening, we found the best restaurant EVER! It was Swiss-style cosy, which means it was beautifully warm and toasty. It also had the deliciously comforting smell of hearty food that nourished the nostrils the moment you walked through the door, and then there was the view, which overlooked all of Verbier. The log fire was roaring and the twinkling lights of hundreds of mountain cabins dotted about in the snowy landscape were like stars puncturing the black velvet night sky. The night was still and the air was dry, and I was struck by the natural freshness of the atmosphere.

We ordered a large pot of cheese fondue and hung out; it was special to spend this time and create these experiences with my mum. It felt good having the time with her and to see her enjoying the finer things in life.

***

The next day, we left the bunker for good and headed to meet the group leader, Stevie. Stevie was a 'lad's lad'. It was obvious from the beginning that the trip was more of a jolly to him than a learning-based experience, as he was more concerned with doing chilli-infused shots at the bar.

Joining us were a cocktail of individuals ranging from 29 to 55 in age; all physiotherapists, all keen to ski and every one of them was passionate about physio. Some were from private practice and others from public health care. I was the youngest of the group by far, but that was fine by me – I was having the time of my life.

As it turned out, Stevie and his newly formed 'crew' of blokes had been out the night before and it was sufficiently 'hardcore' to cause one member to defecate in his bed. It was an interesting way to meet the new group. 'Hi, so you're the guy that shat in the bed last night,' but, hey ho, we were on the trip, so I didn't care (although I was a little surprised that someone on a 'professional development' trip with a group of people who he had never met before would get himself into such a state). Stevie, being the upstanding character that he was, made sure that everyone knew and so rumours about this bed shitter began to swirl.

Stevie was like your typical school bully, and a crew of jock friends began to form around him. Then there was a younger attractive blonde woman, who I could tell had either just come out of a serious relationship or was here to find herself in some way.

It was an abrupt start to the trip. As we marched off in search of the chalet, I wondered what it had in store for us. Clearly, this wasn't going to be the type of ski holiday I had been on with my family in Scotland.

When we finally found the chalet, it was idyllic and led straight out onto the slope. I was given a room on the bottom floor which looked a bit like a bachelor pad.

What I didn't know was that I would be joined later by Stevie's brother, who was also gatecrashing the trip and would act as head chef for the week. Stevie's brother was bunking in my room on a pull-out foldaway bed. He also snored like a rhinoceros with a cold and came down with horrendous flu on day one, so I made a concerted effort to spend as little time in the room as physically possible. This worked in my favour as I planned on being out every night anyway.

That evening, like most of the others, was spent waiting for Stevie's brother to cook up the food, which for someone not in lectures during the day, seemed to take an inordinate amount of time. I think we were all praying he had washed his hands and knew how to cook. There was plenty of red wine being passed around whilst our bellies rumbled. This got the group mingling and a few people dipped in and out to the balcony for cigarettes. All in all, the group was bonding, and a hum of joviality fell across the chalet.

***

The next morning, there were a few sore heads. I was up and out on the slopes early, ready to scout out the best snow and find some adventurous trails.

Up on the mountain, I felt alive. I was in touch with nature and a deep sense of connection to the universal power. Often, it's only when we are surrounded by things bigger than us that we realise the magnificence of the world around us and the opportunity we have just to be alive.

It had been a few years since I had graced a snowboard, and I was happily surprised at the relative ease in which it all came back to me. Muscle memory and the weight distribution that I needed to turn smoothly and not make a pillock of myself kicked in almost instantly.

I sailed off and had a few runs down the most impressive slopes of my life. I got back into my groove and relished the opportunity for more. At about 10am, Mum and a few others bumped into me on the slopes. I think the mandate for the day had gone out, ski in the morning and lectures in the afternoon.

This was great. We enjoyed a few runs together; Mum skiing and me snowboarding. The long slopes in Verbier gave us a real sense of exhilaration and freedom. There were large jumps dotted about every now and then. They were too big for me to even contemplate, but expert boarders kept whizzing over them, pulling 360s and backflips like it was no big deal. Sport is like that, it shows you that just because you can't do it currently and your mind believes it is impossible, that's merely an illusion, and if you need proof, a posse of naysayers will come along to tell you to shove that thought right back where it came from.

Mastering any sport requires discipline and the dogged persistence it takes to keep going despite the falls, torn ligaments and injuries. It requires the ability to tap into your passion and push through the fear. Sport, especially winter sports like skiing and snowboarding, force you to constantly push the mental barriers of what you thought you were capable of.

Unbeknown to me, in a couple of days I was going to face my own challenge. I would walk a thin line on the precipice between life and death, and that would push me both mentally and physically like nothing I had ever experienced before. It was to change my life forever and require me to stretch into the deepest depths of my own abilities and consciousness in order to survive.

As we meandered down the rest of the slope, the sunlight bounced off the snow, lighting it up like a blanket of Swarovski crystals spread across the ground, and the skies painted a bright powder blue as far your eyes can see. It was one of those magical days you never want to forget.

CHAPTER 2

ON THE EDGE: THE DAY IT HAPPENED

IT WAS EARLY in the morning on day three of the trip, and I was already up on the mountain raring to go and ready to explore. The air was fresh and crisp, and the morning sky a deep azure, with the dazzling sun penetrating the glacial landscape and making it shine like a winter wonderland. It was clearly going to be one of those magnificent days on the slopes where you not only get an enviable tan but you also feel on top of the world.

After taking in the sites, I had warmed up on a fun, playful red ski run about three times, so I was already getting more adventurous and increasingly curious each time. I had found my snowboarding legs and muscles that I didn't even know I had were now coming to life.

On my fourth time round, I decided to explore and venture off-piste. I have no idea why, but I felt ready. In my head, I saw myself as a moderately accomplished snowboarder, although I had never been off-piste before and only done five days of actual boarding in the past four years. My enthusiasm and enjoyment were clearly clouding my judgement.

The reality was that my only real experience was in the USA four years prior when I had informed the instructor I was an advanced snowboarder (despite being a complete novice) and, as a result, got put in the advanced class. This meant I spent the week roaming around with a group of fairly decent boarders picking up the sport as I went. It was a great way to accelerate my learning and the trick paid off. Although terrifying at the start, once I'd got a few hours under my belt, it was GAME ON!

But back to Switzerland, upon reflection, I can only think that I must have felt fairly comfortable with how quickly I had mastered the basic flow of moves required to control the board. I wanted to explore what was over the other side of the crest. I didn't intend to go too far; I was just testing the boundaries. I was your typical blue/red run type of skier trying to attempt black runs because they were 'cooler'. Curiosity led the way.

I jumped off from the ski lift and sped off down the mountainside picking up as much momentum as possible so that I could bank left and make it up the steep side of a snow-filled gully and up over the top of a crest. Looking back, I should have probably hiked this bit and given myself time to check out what was waiting for me on the other side. As you can tell, there's a fair bit of reflection going on here for me right now.

I made my way up over the crest of the mountaintop in one smooth motion and carried on away from the main trail, before descending down the slope ahead of me. It didn't even occur to me to check what I was heading into. It looked good, so I went for it.

I began travelling down the slope in front of me, picking up considerable speed, when I suddenly hit sheet black ice.

It happened in an instant, it was far too quick for me to realise what had happened or react, all that gave it away was the change in the sound of the snow turning to sheet ice under my board. It went from making nearly no noise at all to that ominous sound every snowboarder or skier will be familiar with – the loud grating sound that cuts through the air and signals you're out of options and about to lose any semblance of the control you thought you had.

After no more than a millisecond on the steep, icy slope, my board went from under me. I was flipped backwards, thrust hard on to my back, and landed heavily and painfully. It took me a few seconds to gather myself and to fully understand what was happening after the impact of the fall. The ice was hard, really hard. By now I was skidding on my back at real speed, still attached to my board. I figured that the ice patch would end or that the slope would level out and I would eventually come to a standstill, but as I gathered my senses, I realised I was speeding up as I slid down the mountainside on my back and starting to spin out of control. The situation was quickly becoming dire and it started to dawn on me that my initial assessment of the situation had been wrong, very wrong! The slope wasn't levelling out into a smooth horizontal plateau; I wasn't going to come to a standstill. If anything, the longer I spent sliding, the faster I went, and I had no idea what was lying ahead of me, let alone whether I would hit a rock or catch myself on a tree.

I reached out and tried frantically to stop myself moving, but it was no use. The friction from the rough compacted ice and the velocity at which I was now travelling burnt holes through my gloves. I stared at them in disbelief. *Was this really happening?!*

This was when I knew I was in real trouble.

To put this into perspective, I had been unable to control my movements for at least eight or nine seconds. I was now travelling at speed and had no way of slowing myself down. I was at the mercy of the mountain. When you are sliding down a mountainside, it's like being caught in a vortex; the normal rules of physics don't apply. Gravity, speed and force all seem to work in unfamiliar ways.

Finally, using all my might, focus and energy, I managed to regain control and stop the spinning.

Through sheer brute strength, I repositioned myself to face forward again. I was still flat on my back, but now I was falling feet first down the mountainside like I was on a sledge.

It's hard to describe how incredibly difficult this is to do when you are plummeting down a mountainside at serious speed with friction so bad it rips through your clothing and ice so hard it feels like concrete. My heart was beating rapidly, and I felt an intense surge of adrenaline like nothing I had experienced before course through my body. I knew the situation was terrible; I felt it to my core, deep in my bones. My body was shaken, but at least I had stopped spinning and I was now facing the right way (in a logical sense, that is, I am not sure there is any 'right way' for this type of event).

In this moment of clarity, I stared directly forward and I couldn't believe what I saw. It was like my eyes wouldn't register. All that was in front of me – just a few metres away – was a wall of deep blue sky, and I was hurtling straight towards it. And then it hit me, all at once, I realised in an instant that this was the edge of a cliff, the end of the road. I was in big, big trouble.

I had one or two seconds to make a decision. I knew I couldn't stop; I had been trying in vain, but it was no use. I tried to dig the edge of my snowboard into the side of the mountain like a kind of brake, but the ice was too compacted, and I was moving far too fast. To make matters worse, my legs were being restrained by the board and so I had nothing to push against.

I was on a slip 'n' slide towards death, and this looked to be a one-way ticket. It was futile to keep trying to slow down. If anything, it just made matters worse, as it caused my body to spin again. So I gave up completely on that idea even though it was the most logical.

As I wracked my brain as to what I could do, a thought appeared. I realised that the snowboard was the problem. It was keeping my legs outstretched ahead of me in a spread-eagled position. With my legs attached to the board, I couldn't pull them up to stand and I couldn't dig in and use my feet to slow down. As I processed all these thoughts at once, at break-neck speed, instinct just took over.

In a single moment, I made a decision that would save my life. I sat up, bent forward and stretched out both arms as far as I could reach, like a contortionist. I doubled over and reached down to my bindings and unclipped my snowboard, releasing both of my legs in unison.

The decision I had made at the ski rental shop to try Flow bindings had been a good one. (They are quick release bindings as they only have one big strap holding you in, rather than the standard two straps, meaning that I could release myself from the snowboard's grasp in one singular swift motion.)

This is an important detail because as soon as I unclipped my board, the cliff edge presented itself. It was now or never. I had one final second to think of my next move before it would be over (pardon the pun). By a stroke of inconceivably incredible luck, there was a rock sticking out of the ice slope before the cliff edge to my right-hand side. It was about the size of a bin bag full of garbage. That's the best way I can think to describe it. It wasn't huge, or special in any way, other than the fact that it was there, providing me with an opportunity to save myself from the jaws of death with only a second to spare. With everything in me, all my strength, commitment and instinct, I forced my body to sit in the upright position and, in an instant, launched myself at the rocky boulder. This movement was made possible now that I was free from the burden of the snowboard that had been significantly restricting my movements thus far. I used the momentum of my downward trajectory to the full, leaping like a frog from a pan of boiling water, and pushed myself through the air. I landed with my stomach squarely on the centre of the rock, my arms wrapped around the base and dug in tight, gripping the sides and praying that I had enough strength to hold on. In a moment like this, leaping towards what looks like safety, you pray that once you land, your momentum will cease, and you won't ricochet off or misjudge the distance and overshoot it.

As my arms clung to the rock, my legs were flung off the edge of the cliff. My body and head were now facing up towards the mountain top, and both of my legs were hanging over the edge and pointing down into nothingness. It all happened in an instant. My snowboard shot off the edge of the cliff and down into the blue abyss below.

As I clung on to this miraculous rock, keeping the full weight of my body pushing down through my chest, I turned my head and looked over my shoulder, down below. My legs were still dangling over the side of the cliff and I had to really crane my neck to look backwards.

What I saw changed my life.

My snowboard was still falling through the air, one second, two seconds, three seconds… Time stood still as I watched it crash into the rocks below and bounce off. Then it just kept on going, travelling through the powder.

If any of the events I've just described had happened just a fraction of a second later, I would have been sent over the cliff edge with my board. Just like that, I would have been gone.

I was stunned. There was no way I would have survived a fall like that. By my estimation, it was at least 200 feet.

Lesson 1: Put the plan into action

Had I not put the plan into action and released the snowboard attached to my feet, it is very likely I would have died on that fateful day only a few moments later. To come that close to death and not take away the lesson would have been a real mistake: putting my plan into action saved me.

Not taking action would have kept me bound in a horizontal position, sliding down the mountainside with no way of stopping and nothing firm to either dig the snowboard into or push against, as a result of the gravitational pull and my outstretched position. Staying stuck in this perilous predicament meant I wouldn't have been able to launch myself on to the rock and the opportunity for survival would have passed me by, quite literally.

Even if, by sheer luck, I had managed to hold on to something substantial to slow myself down (depending on how my legs twisted as the board went over the cliff edge), it could have pulled me over the top with it, causing me fall to my inevitable death, or made it incredibly difficult to hold on to anything, again causing me to slip and freefall to oblivion.

It gives me shivers down my spine just writing about it. **I cannot stress this enough: in decision-making, procrastination is death.**

I know that not all decisions are quite as life and death as this, but due to this specific experience, I believe the most effective decision-makers make decisions quickly and then commit to carrying them out. Decisiveness is the trait of a true leader and this lesson has helped me out in multiple situations in life since that fateful day. I am sharing this with you in the hope that this lesson will serve you too.

Trapped in such an extreme situation, it would have been futile to just have the thought and not put the plan into action. Its value was unlocked by my implementation of the act when the idea was transformed into a real lifesaving outcome.

It was like a force came over my body and just made me act. Instinct, intuition, divine guidance, made me reach down, unclip the board, before I turned and threw myself towards the large rock. Miraculously, it was the only one free of any snow coverage so I could see it and, divinely, it was only 3-4 feet away, perched exactly on the edge of the cliff I was about to slide off.

Lesson 1 summary:

- There is a cost to inaction.
- Making no decision is still making a decision.
- Even when you cannot be 100% sure and the stakes are high, it is better to make a

> decision and commit to carrying it out than just doing nothing.

As I clung onto the rock and contemplated what to do next, a sensation of deep calm and control came over me. I knew that this was it, any decision I made going forward would either lead to my very quick death or my survival.

When you get this close to the edge of life, you achieve great clarity in the mind. It's the clearest and most focused I have ever been. I can say that without a doubt. There was no margin for error, just black and white, life or death.

I said out loud to myself, 'Tim, do not mess this up.' I was giving myself the pep talk of my life. Not having been in a cliffhanger situation before, it felt like the right thing to do. Talking to myself allowed me to make sense of the ordeal and stay present in the moment. It also made me feel less alone and gave me hope that there was a way out of this. I had suffered an incredibly close brush with death and yet, I was still alive and could choose how the next steps would play out.

Lesson 2: The power of pep talks

Verbalising what you are thinking allows you to quickly take control of your mind. It might sound strange, but as a teenage guy but as a teenage guy who'd grown up skateboarding, listening to punk rock bands like Blink-182 and watching shows like *Jackass* with Johnny Knoxville, I remember warning myself away from thinking this was funny and to take it seriously. Somewhere in my teenage mind, I could imagine myself saying, 'Dude, gnarly fall.'

Hence why the first words out of my mouth were: 'Tim, do not mess this up.' My inner self was leading, taking control. Now, I had found my groove there was no chance of Immature Tim making an appearance. It was all Leader Tim.

I needed to get my mind right so that I could make life-saving decisions. Gaining control of my thoughts and taking command of my mind was imperative. The pep talk, which was driven by some internal force and came out of nowhere, gave me the sense of being a friend to myself, and it was in this dialogue I clearly mapped out what to do next.

My focus was on not making any rash decisions or rushing and then slipping and falling. I was conscious that I needed to be extra careful not to make the situation any worse than it already was – hanging 200 feet above a sheer drop onto a pile of jagged rocks in the middle of a snowy outback somewhere off-piste in Switzerland, with no phone or food. The pep talk allowed me to control the pace of my mind and slowly think out each action.

When you need to take control of a situation, talk it out. Give yourself a pep talk and set out what options you have. This keeps your mind focused on what's in front of you.

Lesson 2 summary:

- Talking to yourself gives you the chance to discuss/debate both sides of the argument.

- You can improve your mindset with positive self-talk, just as you can destroy your mindset with negative self-talk.

- Taking control of your mind is a key step to helping you weigh up the options.

After a few moments, I shifted my weight and centralised my body on the rock. I pulled myself up slowly and sat with my knees around the base of the rock, straddling it. Adrenaline was coursing through my body. I felt physically strong, but I also knew that any wrong decision would take my life away from me at any second. I was acutely aware of the possibility of this becoming a grave reality. Behind me was the vast expanse of 200 feet of nothingness and in front of me was the steep hard icy death trap that I had just triumphed over.

Danger was looming all around me, and yet I felt calm, clear-headed and mentally strong enough to

figure this out. Having had my life saved, I wasn't going to give up without a fight.

The only options I had were to either stay on the rock, praying that I didn't get tired and cold, or slip off the edge whilst I waited in hope that someone somewhere would find me. This was before the days of smartphones and ski suits with GPS tracking built into them.

No one knew where I was for the day. The rest of the crew were in lectures, so I anticipated that it would be at least a few hours, if not nightfall, before my disappearance was apparent, and even then, how would they know where to begin their search? This mountain was unlikely to be the first place they would think to look for me.

The other option I had was to try and make it over to the left side of the clifftop. I could see a huge pile of boulders about 15-20 metres away, each about the size of a car, that cascaded down the side of the mountain like a gigantic landslide.

If I could make it over to them, I could potentially slowly climb down the boulder pile. This wouldn't be without its challenges, of course, but I had to try, especially if it was a route down to safety. I couldn't go back up the slope to where I came from. If I put one foot on the sheet ice, I would slip over the edge, plummeting to an instant death. I had to find a relatively safe way down and at least this option got me out of the immediate danger of sitting on the edge of the cliff. As long as I didn't put myself in a worse situation, I might have a chance of getting off the mountain alive. The question was, could I make it across the crest of the cliff unscathed?

I decided that crossing the cliff face was the way forward, as sitting on the rock left me in extreme danger. If I could make it across the mouth of the cliff and over the pile of rocks, I could decrease the risk of immense danger. My thinking was, if I could take it slow, it might be possible to inch my way across. This would take focus and dexterity but it looked and felt possible, so I decided to go for it.

Lesson 3: Prioritise fast

I had to make a decision. Remember, that making no decision is still making a decision. Any number of things could have happened if I'd stayed precariously perched on the rock. There could have been an avalanche, or the weather could have turned rapidly. I could not risk being stuck in a storm, vulnerable to the forces of nature, and blown off the cliff face. Given the temperature, I couldn't have survived on that rock for long.

Alternatively, I could have attempted to make it steadily across the cliff face. Walking across the edge of a cliff was not something I wanted to do; after all, one wrong step and I would have been dead. But with no phone and the imminent danger I was in, I decided it was worth the risk; otherwise, I could die on that rock. This shift in perspective allowed me to weigh up the options based on future potential outcomes.

If I was successful, the downside was that I would be less visible on the cliffside than where I was currently positioned in the middle. It was my responsibility to weigh up all the options and then make the decision to execute a plan to the best of my ability.

Remember, committing to a plan doesn't mean that you can't change your mind if new information presents itself. It just means that you are taking a careful assessment of the surroundings and doing what you perceive to be the best option given the circumstances.

Sliding towards the cliff edge

Another occasion when I'd been forced to reprioritise rapidly, as new information presented itself, was when I realised I was heading towards a cliff with an unknown drop. I needed to reprioritise and change my approach to the situation.

Taking the board off hadn't occurred to me before then due to my reluctance to lose the board. However, when the situation suddenly changed and new information presented itself, losing my board became totally insignificant, as it was the obvious choice.

Notice how we are blocked from ideas based on the information, context and stimuli around us. When you uncover new information, like the emergence of the cliff edge, your priorities and strategies must change.

In comparison to my life, the board was nothing. **This is a key distinction in decision-making – we can be flexible, at any time, in moving the components that enable us to play out different scenarios**. Had I thought about taking the board off earlier, before I had reached the edge, maybe I could have stopped myself sooner.

Lesson 3 summary:

- You rarely have all the information imaginable, but you have to prioritise, based on what you have.

- Rationally weigh up the options, decide what is most important and let that be your guide.

- Be flexible in your approach as the situation and context changes. If it's not working, change it, listen to the feedback of failure and find a strategy that works.

I committed to action. As I stood up on the rock, I knew the next few minutes were critical. My mind was crystal clear on the mission at hand.

As I delicately sank my right foot into the snow next to the rock, I prayed that as I put my weight down, I wouldn't touch the ice, as this would cause me to lose my balance and slip. Walking this route on the precipice was like walking the fine line between life and death. My heart was in my mouth as my foot touched the hard snowy surface below. No ice. My mind was razor-sharp. I focused on gently shifting my weight onto my right foot. I was most afraid of the snow breaking off from the cliff edge and me going overboard with it.

All my energy was focused on establishing each slow step; first gently putting my foot down and then transferring my full weight down. Each step took me closer to my goal of getting to the other side. With every step, I made sure I was balanced correctly, with even pressure and weight distribution, so that I didn't topple over.

Lesson 4: Focus or fail

Have you ever noticed that when two joggers pass each other in opposite directions on the sidewalk, they nearly collide into each other even though there is more than enough space on either side of them? This strange phenomenon occurs because although they are focused on *not* hitting the other person, they are looking the other person in the eyes, and so their bodies move in that direction and bam!

We get what we focus on. You might have experienced this yourself when you're jogging. The real way to avoid the other person is to focus on where you want to go, and not on where you don't.

Somewhere between my saving grace (the rock) and the boulders ahead, I began to feel a sense a slight relief, a lifting of the weight, as there was no turning back now. No second guessing, every step, every movement, every breath had to be calculated and perfectly executed. There was a rhythm to it, underpinned by a deep focus that took concentrated effort.

As I walked along the edge of the cliff, there was a 200-foot drop to the left and an icy death trap of a slope to my right. Not knowing if my next step would be fatal, my body became my sensory guide. It had superpowers when it came to detecting the speed of the wind, the glare of the sunlight, the distracting noises, the sound of the snow crunching under foot and measuring the depth of each step as it sank and took my body weight.

My body became the optimisation centre, the computer, relying solely on my gut instinct and listening to all the feedback around me, and what it was telling me.

Stopping to overanalyse the motion would have broken the spell, so the only way to succeed was to continue. I was hyper aware that stopping for a rest might make me disorientated, lose my footing and topple over to the side in either direction, which would have meant the end. This task, although death-defyingly scary, had to be carried out in its entirety until it was completed. There was no room for anything else. The lesson here was to focus solely on where I wanted to go, reject all distractions and analyse all the feedback I could get from the world around me.

It would have been easy to get distracted, to lose concentration, but to do so even for a second would have put my life in grave danger. If I wanted to see another day, my only option was to focus entirely on what mattered to get the job done right.

Lesson 4 summary:

- If you focus on the outcome you don't want, that is what will happen.
- Concentrate on achieving your goal, one step at a time.
- Stay present and focus on what matters.

Right foot, left foot, right foot, left foot, this was the most important walk of my life. Each step felt like I was pushing through a boundary of the unknown. Every step took me closer to safety. I had to focus only on reaching the other side, and not look to my left for even one split second, and focus on the 200-foot drop below. If I allowed my mind to go there, it would surely be over. Every cell in my body knew this. The fight was won in my mind. I would not let myself look. I would not let this unprecedented turn of events and truly out of this world experience take precedence. If I let it fuel my curiosity, even for a second, that would be it.

I became aware, through my peripheral vision, that small streams of snow were rushing off the edge, down into the abyss below, but I stopped myself from looking, as that would mean giving in and I had already said 'no' to that option. I had to just keep focused on reaching the other side, step by careful step.

After fifteen, maybe twenty minutes, I had made the final few steps and reached the side of the cliff. I was now at the top of the cascade of boulders that pointed down the side of the mountain. I had made it. Time seemed to slow down.

Inside, I don't remember celebrating, but I do remember a deep sense of calmness despite understanding how dire my situation was. The stakes were the highest I had ever encountered. I had not experienced life in this form before. Every decision needed to be cross-referenced, checked and acted upon.

Due to the nature of the mountain, I was well aware that conditions could change in an instant. Now I was out of immediate danger, but I still had to deal with getting down or spending the night on the mountain in sub-zero temperatures, with no food, shelter or warmth. This is where my mindset was key to keeping me focused on the goal at hand. Staying alive!

CHAPTER 3

THE CAVE AND THE COURAGE TO KNOW THE WAY FORWARD

I MADE THE decision to try and get off the mountain whilst I had the energy and it was still daylight with fine sunny conditions. As I looked down the cliffside, I noticed that some of the rocks and boulders descended down into what looked like a big dark cave, the entrance of which was large enough and near enough for me to climb down into. My biggest concern now was making sure that whatever I did, I could still get back to this point at the side of the cliff. The journey began with my decision to press forward.

I determined that I should go down and explore the cave, and that it was worth the risk if it took me closer to the bottom of the mountain.

This was where I stepped into the unknown and trusted my gut instinct again. Thinking back, I was drawn to the cave, I felt led. Having made it across the cliff edge and been spared the fall, I had to try and go down. The worst-case scenario was

> **that I would make it back up to the cave and wait there for someone to find me.**

My gut told me that exploring the cave would be a safer route than continuing further down the vertical cliff face by going over the top of the boulders. One false move and I'd be gone.

To give you an idea, the cave was located roughly 20 metres away from my current position; not far, but given the treacherous terrain and inhospitable environment that surrounded me, the route down needed careful consideration.

Lesson 5: Future-oriented optimism

In a sense, I allowed the future of what I wanted come into the present situation. I began with the end in mind. I was fully present, acting in the spirit of the future I wanted to create, which was to free myself from this ordeal, get back to safety and live out the rest of my life.

When I look back now and think about the enormity of what I could have missed out on if I had died on the mountain, it terrifies me: not meeting and falling in love with my wife; not experiencing the joy of being a father or witnessing my baby's first steps, first words, first smile; not being able to see my children grow up and hold them in my arms; never drumming or playing guitar again, not seeing my favourite bands perform at Nottingham Rock City; never reaching the sunny beaches of Thailand, and not fulfilling my purpose on this Earth.

I was making decisions based on the belief that I could free myself from this near-death experience I found myself in. My mind was free to think creatively and act independently from the burden I was surrounded by. I could make sense of the situation by looking forward to where I wanted to get to and then plan how to get there.

This practice helped me to avoid disaster and steer clear from panic or giving into my emotions. By focusing on what I wanted, e.g. to get off the mountain, and working backwards from that point, I ended up breaking the problem down into smaller goals. This gave me a series of mini challenges to overcome, and as soon as one mini challenge was accomplished, I decided how best to handle the next one. This meant I only ever focused on the present challenge (not the next one or the next one). This balance between the present and the future goal gave me perspective and allowed me to focus my energy on progressing forward, so I remained in 'solution mode' and did not entertain any thought of defeat.

In order to get to the mouth of the cave, I still had to clamber along the top of 3-4 gigantic icy boulders in my big size 11 cumbersome snowboard boots, with next to no grip. I had to be extra careful that I didn't slip and break an arm or a leg (significantly decreasing my chances of survival in the process).

The rocks were perilous and unforgiving, wrapped in a layer of ice that was covered by a layer of snow which disguised their deathly threat. It was another make or break moment. I was putting my life in my own hands climbing over the ridge of these rocks. I had to summon the mental fortitude to ensure that my body was fully supported by my grip and that no matter how long it took, I didn't slip and injure myself. To do so would most likely seal my fate.

It's strange to reflect on that moment, but looking at it in terms of the bigger picture now (which I have the privilege to do, sitting here at 6.35am, writing this book from the comfort of my office), it's strange to think that to get to the supposed cave (remember I had no confirmation of what it was yet), I had to go through another test. To me, this is a very real example of the laws of life and nature intertwining. I needed to trust my instinct enough to explore, trust my body enough to carry me to safety and trust my mind to be resilient enough to cope with the extreme situation. Remember, all the time this was occurring I was still balancing the anxiety from my building adrenaline and the pressure to get off the mountain before nightfall. On top of all of that, I was acutely reminded of the very real danger every time I looked forward and began my descent down. No ropes, no food, no prior mountaineering experience, it was just me and the elements up there.

This fork in the road describes the constant interplay that takes place between making a decision and weighing up the options. Because I had decided to get off the mountain ASAP, rather than stay on the rock that had saved my life, I was exploring unknown terrain. This could shift at any moment and leave me trapped, injured or worse. It was an experiment of the greatest proportions. I had to balance my desire to get off the mountain as quickly as possible, whilst I still had the energy, with heeding caution when it was needed at the expense of progress, all the while acting with dexterity. In this way, progress was making the right decision and delivering the appropriate response, no matter if it ate up time or expended energy.

There were sections of the rock face that took much longer to navigate than others. Going over boulders was nerve-rackingly dangerous; one false move could have seen me lose control and fall forward down into the vast chasm below or fall backwards and cause a fatal injury.

To complicate matters (not that I had the chance to focus on it for too long due to the abundance of adrenaline that was surging powerfully through my body), I didn't have any food on me. This meant that I was running purely on adrenaline. With no food and the knowledge that my energy was depleting by the second, I made the decision to go for it and use my energy stores, which were now enhanced by the adrenaline spike, to do everything in my power to find a way down. This meant fuelling my mind to come up with creative ideas, problem-solving and pushing myself harder than I had ever done before.

The problem with 100% adrenaline energy is that it makes you slightly jumpy, like a motorbike that revs away before a race, wanting – no, begging – for the brake to be released. This means that, ironically, you spend more energy on keeping your movement smooth and calibrated, as you have to fight the vigorous, explosive and uncontrolled energy inside you.

I made fast progress dropping down from the boulders and rocky ledges. My only concern at this time was landing safely and not twisting an ankle in haste, while maintaining the ability to go back up if necessary should I reach a dead-end.

With each stage of the descent, I made sure that I could get back up. Literally testing out the route as I went, going one or two steps down then four steps back up, rehearsing the route.

I decided that I would go forward until I reached a point where there came a fork in the road in the form of a drop that was too big for me to climb back up. This fork in the road would have required me to make an irreversible decision. Luckily, that moment never came. I was always able to find a way back up if necessary and I could always find a route with drops that were five feet or less.

Once I had clambered over a big section of daunting rocks and ice, I reached the mouth of the crevasse or 'cave'. Let's call it a cave, although this wasn't a cave in the typical sense of the word. I imagine a cave to be formed through the weathering of rock over the years or chiselled out by human effort. This cave was created by fallen rock, and then haphazardly put together by Mother Nature, and I was uncertain that it was even stable. I knew I was about to enter a turning point which could either lead to my survival or my end.

Entering this dark cave-like rock formation, I wasn't sure what lay ahead of me, or if the whole structure would collapse at any moment, trapping me inside or worse. By going into the cave, I was taking myself completely off the grid and reducing my chances of being spotted to zero, but it felt right to explore, even though I understood this was a potentially fatal risk.

I can't explain it, other than to say it felt like I was called to it, draw in by the hope of a way forward that wouldn't involve me going over the top of the rocks further, where gravity would pull me hazardously. (To give you context, there were two options at this stage, continue over the top of the cave and crawl over icy rocks and ledges at a near 65-70-degree angle, or go explore inside the cave.) The cave felt like a safe haven, a break from the cold vast winter landscape outside and would at least provide me with some shelter from the elements.

I was surprised by the sheer darkness inside. It took a good thirty seconds for my eyes to adjust from the bright luminous snowscape outside to the complete and utter darkness. Then, out of nowhere, *smack*! I bumped my head into a rock pointing directly at my crown. I was moving too quickly, the cave, despite looking like a shield from the freezing cold and wind, had its own myriad of challenges. New ones that I would have to learn.

Whereas outside, I had had the advantage of light, in here, I was sealed off from the world and any accident, any call for help, any avalanche, and it could be game over. I needed to adapt my movements to the style of the environment and give myself time to adjust, whilst also staying focused and alert for any hidden obstacles and pitfalls. I knew the stakes were high and I needed to reach inside and draw out all the determination, creativity and energy inside myself to figure a way out of this. I had to control my emotions and thoughts in this way; if I didn't, I would be walking headfirst into disaster.

I didn't know it then, but this would be the first and the last trip that I would get to take with my mum (she sadly passed away two years later due to a malignant and rapid form of skin cancer that took us all by surprise. She was taken from this Earth but she had other work to do).

Finding the drive to get myself out served a higher purpose. Finding that fire inside of me to figure a way out so that I could complete this trip with her and build memories that would stay with me beyond her passing just two years later was a must.

There was a fire there and it was at the front leading the experience. Giving up was never an option. I had made the decision. It never crossed my mind to give up, even when I was climbing through this maze of sharp jagged rocks into potential oblivion.

My mindset was my greatest weapon and in order to succeed, I had to hold firm. There was something greater driving my decisions, the severity and consequences allowed me to operate in a high-performance state, constantly observing the changing environment and rapidly shifting my approach to best navigate it. I was operating on a knife-edge, my senses were resolute, I was in flow, making decisions and committing to them.

Lesson 6: Don't give in to your fears

People speak of fight or flight mode, the psychology behind decision-making, but in this state of high-pressure decision-making, I was in a new realm of action. I made a decision, committed, and then acted. It was as if I was at one with the mountain and the situation that I had to overcome. I had to claw back my life from the jaws of death, which were staring at me, waiting for me to make a false step, but I wasn't going to let that happen.

I didn't question my decisions or experience fear like I thought I would. After sliding down the mountainside towards death and then surviving, the rush was so great that anything from now on was going to be a win. I did not allow myself to think of the worst-case scenario and remained positive that taking action and exploring was the correct course and this kept my spirits high. By having the courage to explore, rather than sit it out on the top of the cliff and hope I was spotted, I gained some sense of control in an incredibly extreme, inconceivable and challenging situation.

I was in a state of solid positivity and the very fact that my life was on a knife-edge was a strong motivator to stay in this state. To give in to fear or question my next move would have led to decision paralysis and panic. Questioning my decisions for too long and over-rationalising would also have led to dire consequences.

For example, playing it too safe would have held me back from my ultimate objective of getting down the cliff and finding my way back home. It was as if my mind and body, my inner self, my very person had taken over without me consciously thinking about it. I was able to operate in this balanced state, observing all that was around me in the environment, making a decision and then taking exceptionally calculated action.

Lesson 6 summary:

- Fear can derail your decision-making process.

- Once you have made a decision, do not question it, do not let in those nagging doubts. Keep pressing forward.

During some of the more challenging sections, I had to get down on my hands and knees and lie flat on my belly to crawl under and through tight gaps in the rocks to progress to where I could see the light coming from.

With every step, I was moving further into the unknown. In that cave, I was more aware than ever that if something happened, no one would find me.

Through all of this, I felt clear-headed and positive about the possibilities of where the cave might lead.

This growth mindset kept me scanning the rocky landscape for opportunities.

Lesson 7: Get creative at problem-solving

To make progress, I needed to get creative.

There were times when I had to hang and then drop down large crevasses in the darkness, feeling my way along in the damp and cold structure. Mentally, I weighed up every eventuality. As I did so, options seemed to appear out of nowhere and suddenly, as if by magic, I would find a way to get over or around an obstacle, which didn't seem previously possible.

I knew something inside of myself wouldn't let me give up. It was like an inner voice that kept me going, searching for new routes and new possibilities. I had an awareness and knew that if I just kept going, I would figure it out, whatever it was that stood in my way. If I remained alert and on the ball I could avoid increasing the potential danger I was in.

In the cave, I knew that every downward step took me away from the light above but closer to my goal, which was to explore what was at the bottom and see if I could find an exit that came out lower down the cliff. The cave had clearly been formed by a major landslide, which meant that it should lead me to the bottom of the cliff.

However, there was a strong probability that it was formed by a landslide, which meant that it would be unstable. One wrong move could see me trapped. This increased the magnitude of the situation tenfold.

My survival depended on the quality of the decisions I made. Bringing creativity into the equation allowed me to multiply the effectiveness of each decision. Think of creativity as a catalyst. Whether you are in business or stuck on the side of a cliff in the snowy mountains of Switzerland, creativity has a place in decision-making and problem-solving.

It was the ability to weave ideas together, play out scenarios in advance and visualise the unseen in my mind's eye that allowed me safe passage through the cave. When you're that deep in the darkness, alone and unsure, creativity is like the guiding light of your soul, keeping the walls of impending doom at bay and prodding you to put one foot in front of the other. The human mind is a brilliant thing, for within it is the capacity to withstand more than you think is possible, and come up with solutions to anything. When challenged to rise to the occasion, with potential death on the other side of the bargaining table, I was compelled to play to my strengths.

In order to increase the potency of the creative problem-solving session I was hosting in the cave, I had to let my mind run freer, and operate outside of the constraints of the current environment, with questions such as:

- If I was able to squeeze under this tight gap in the rock, how would I do it?
- What do I need to consider before I do it?
- How can I mitigate the risks?
- What are the alternatives?
- What is the worst that can happen?
- Where have I seen something like this before?
- What does success look like? Can I emulate it?
- If I wasn't in a cave, how would I approach this?
- What could be on the other side?

Questions such as these liberated me from the normal neural pathways and opened up the possibility of overcoming the hurdles, time after time. It is important to mention and reiterate the role of hope, faith and belief in this process. The creative ideation process that I used was generally optimistic, but with an undertone of realism around what could go wrong. I would estimate a 90% positive/10% extreme negative influence. This allowed my mental reserves to properly meld together my ideas and tap into my creative reservoir.

Lesson 7 summary:

- When you are up against it, give your mind the freedom to point out creative solutions.

- Panic and fear will kill your ability to problem-solve creatively.

- Ask yourself questions to promote creative thinking.

As well as using my creativity, I needed a boost to ensure my survival, something extra, a helping hand from God. In a situation like this, where I was up against the clock, attempting to figure a way out of this before nightfall or a change in the weather, the precipice between life and death was clearer, more distinct. In fact, I could see it. Death was all around me in the cave. If I hit my head or became disorientated in the darkness and forgot my way out, the end would be imminent. On the cliff edge, if I had toppled over or slipped due to a momentary lapse in concentration, death would have won. But in my heightened state of consciousness, I had a very real connection with God, like he was on speed dial and providing a protective aura around me that kept me out of harm's way. In the lesson below, I will share with you why this direct lifeline of communication was important and how faith played a crucial role.

Lesson 8: Faith matters

The mind is one of the most powerful tools we have, if not the most powerful. If we give in to the external reality of the situation and allow the negative voice inside our heads to exert its dominance, the mind becomes confused and takes us off course. We experience negative thoughts and start to believe that things aren't possible, and our focus is redirected away from taking inspired action, invigorating faith and a world of possibility. To keep my faith strong, I prayed to God. I talked to myself in an upbeat manner and I told myself that I was here on this Earth for a purpose and that I wasn't going to die up here on the mountain. I simply wouldn't let that be my fate. I would find a way.

Overthinking and negative thinking would have led me quickly down a slippery slope (pardon the pun). If I had indulged my urges to follow these thoughts, it would have taken my attention away from the task at hand, which would have been a catastrophic mistake, however easy it would have been to indulge.

At times during the ordeal, I remember thinking about the intense severity of my situation, being off-piste in unknown mountainous terrain, with only four hours before the freezing night sky rolled in and the environment became unbearable. But the key to survival was that I killed the negative thought as soon as it occurred. It was fleeting, and I killed it in the instant it showed up. I had full confidence in my quest to keep trying whilst I had the energy. I knew these first few hours were crucial and reasoned it couldn't get better than this, so this was my best opportunity to focus my senses and attention on finding a way out.

Throughout, I would talk out loud to God and pray he would keep me safe, especially in the cave and when I felt the enormity of the situation was becoming too daunting. After all, when I was sliding down the mountainside, something had told me to focus on not spinning and to get my body under control. This thought, which I acted upon, allowed me to see what was coming ahead (the edge of a vertical 200-foot cliff) and course-correct before I went over the edge (unclipping the board and leaping towards a rock) at the exact time I needed to, with not even a millisecond to spare. Something forced me to reach down and unclip my bindings and release the snowboard, and then, miraculously, I just happened to be sliding towards the only area of the cliff edge where there was a rock sticking out, as if placed there by divine intervention for me to throw myself at. It was as if someone, the universe or God, was watching out for me.

I felt all the decisions that I made were guided by a force greater than myself. The clarity of mind, the speed of understanding and the determination to see it through, whatever it took, when I was clinging on to the rock was out of this world. I didn't even think about slipping. I thought about making the right next move. I was considered, calm and present and that was the demeanour I maintained throughout the ordeal. God was driving my every move, allowing me to spot the opportunity and act on it with commitment and decisiveness. My resourcefulness was abundant, overflowing and creative, and although I had a deep understanding of how grave the situation was, I was flabbergasted at the unbelievable speed at which life changes in an instant. I knew that it was me and God up there on the mountain.

Having faith gave me resilience when the problems in front of me seemed too big. It gave me courage in the darkness. It showed me there was more to life and more at work here and by trusting my guide, I had a helping hand. Faith saved me as it gave me the presence of thought, clarity of mind and held me safely as it guided me through this maze of catastrophe. It would have been easy to die up there on the mountain, if I had given in to my emotions, if I hadn't listened to the calling and allowed a deeper awareness to lead.

Lesson 8 summary:

- Faith (or lack of it) impacts both your thinking and your actions, and ultimately the outcomes you achieve.

- In life, when important decisions need to be made, first become clear on what your goal is and find a spot to meditate or get some peace. Allow yourself to be centred. What is your mind's eye guiding you to do? Being at one with a high state of consciousness can be one of the best ways to make great decisions because you act on these decisions with more confidence, conviction and knowing. It is an inner knowing that a force greater than you is at work.

There were times in the cave when the darkness seemed to surround me more than others, when I could only see a couple of feet in front and wondered if I would ever make it out the other side or if there was even an exit. Again, I didn't let this monster of a thought grow. I culled it before it had a chance to expand, as if I was observing it, taking note and moving on.

I used the adrenaline from the near-death cliffhanger to fuel my focus and then leveraged the calmness I was experiencing to aid my analysis, detection and creative thinking. At one stage, I had to bend down and lie flat on my stomach to roll under a piece of hanging rock. It was a frighteningly tight space and I felt claustrophobia and panic rise up in me for a second, before picking myself up and carrying on.

Even though I was making progress by moving down the cliff face. I was unsure whether I was actually making real progress or just heading deeper into a dark crevasse and wasting valuable (lifesaving) time. When I think about it, it was a big risk. I was either walking myself towards death or survival.

It felt good when I had little wins, but with each decision and each move, I remained fully focused on the next move ahead and the changing reality I faced. In my mind, it was not over until I reached the outside world again at the bottom and I stood looking up at what I had overcome. This concentrated mindset and focus were key to keeping my mind sharp and on task.

CHAPTER 4

THE LIGHT OF LOVE

AFTER ROUGHLY THREE hours of my descent into the cave, I finally saw it. A bright white shining hole was pouring light into the darkness. It was sunlight bouncing off snow. It was the outside world. I didn't know it yet, but I had reached the foot of the cliff. The light was piercing the darkness with a radiance that felt like love.

Somehow, I had been led to this small opening at the very bottom of the cave. To get to this point, I had been forced to step blindly into the unknown with faith and trust that I would make the right decision. As I reached the light, I saw a small doorway to freedom. It was absolutely tiny, about the size of my head, but it was a gap in the rocks that shone brightly. Ironically, it was the darkness that allowed me to see this light. Had it been a chasm lit with daylight then this exit wouldn't have been so apparent; in fact, I might have missed it altogether. But here, the thick blanket of darkness gave me the opportunity to spot my way out. The small rays of sunlight cut through like lasers with a warm glow that invited me to bend down and explore. The beams of light were streaming through at my feet. I got down onto my hands and knees and felt around. It was a familiar feeling; it was compacted snow. Not as hard as on the icy mountainside I'd been snowboarding on a few hours earlier. It was firm, crisp snow.

I dug away some of the snow around the hole with my friction-burnt gloves, my raw skin now showing through the holes. I kept digging, and as I did, more light poured into the cave. My confidence grew and elation filled my heart as the light filled the bottom of the cave around me. The hole I had created was not big, about 2 feet wide by 1.5 feet high. Would I fit through it? I didn't stop to think too long about it. As I pushed my head through, I prayed that I could fit through the gap in the cave wall that I had uncovered.

Again, this was another moment where I reckon I would have got stuck if I had stopped to think about it for too long, or been overcome with decision paralysis about how best to fit through the gap. The thing that got me through was my faith and mindset. I chose not to focus on the claustrophobia of the tiny gap I was attempting to force myself through and, instead, I became supple, adaptable and moved at speed. I did not allow my mind to entertain thoughts of failure. I didn't contemplate not getting through to the other side or getting stuck midway through. I believe it was this combination of flexibility and persistence that carried me through to the other side and freedom.

As I crawled out into almost blinding sunlight, I realised I had done it. I had walked on the precipice between life and death, trusted my deepest instincts and been guided down a cliff face across inhospitable terrain into the unknown, and all the time I had been working to a tight deadline (e.g. before nightfall, before my energy ran out and my body became weaker, before my thoughts and judgement clouded, before the freezing winter sky darkened).

Moving as fast as I could, I made my way around the vast expanse of fallen rocks at the bottom of the landslide. The rocks ranged from the size of an SUV to a minibus. I was trudging through deep untouched powder and up to my thighs in snow. It was hard work to plough on, as the snow sucked each leg down. I staggered purposefully around the base of the landslide of rocks to look upon the size of the cliff I had just climbed down.

In that moment, I craned my head back to take it all in. What I saw took my breath away. The huge scale of what I had achieved appeared to me in its fullest revelation yet. I realised the drop was much, much bigger than I had previously thought. Remember, I had not allowed myself to look down during my climb.

There was absolutely no way I would have made the fall – it led directly on to rocks. It must have been a 400-foot drop with no second chances.

I gazed up at the sheer scale of the cliff in front of me, but didn't pause for long to contemplate. I was keen to keep going and reach civilisation again, but that image and experience has stayed with me. It is etched on my mind forever.

I decided to follow the tracks that my snowboard had made in the pristine white snow in the hope of locating it, so that I could scoot across the snow instead of pounding step after step along the nearly flat land. Moments later, I found it further down the mountain. It hadn't travelled too far but had a few large cracks in the nose to show for its tale of sailing off the cliff.

Key Lessons Summary:

1. Put the plan into action

Ideas pop into our heads for a reason; they are the starting point of achieving what we want. Desires must be translated into action for them to have any effect. Sometimes, ideas are guided by forces greater than ourselves and appear as if by magic at the exact moment we need them. Do not let these opportunities pass. In business or in your personal life, putting the plan into action is the key to all great things. An oak tree only becomes large because the acorn unlocks its potential through action.

2. The power of pep talks

When facing high-stake situations and making decisions under pressure, do not underestimate the power of a pep talk. It's the reason the super successful have coaches. Pep talks are a fantastic way to control your thought and refocus your mind on what really matters. Incantations, mantras and positive self-talk are all necessary ways to help you make better, less irrational decisions. Get closer to the power of positivity and joy and you'll find that your decision-making becomes simpler, more aligned and produces world-class results.

3. Prioritise fast

If I had not made the decision to take my snowboard off, or focus my energy on not spinning around so that I could see what was coming, I would not be here today. Information is changing all the time, and you need to make critical decisions based on what is of the most importance.

4. Focus or fail

I had absolute **certainty** and **clarity** that **I would do everything in my power** to make it out of the situation alive by using creativity, determination and mindset. Managing my emotions played a big part in maintaining a mindset that filled me with hope and kept me open to opportunities, and meant I was able to implement and test strategies to get down the cliff in one piece.

5. Future-orientated optimism

Being mentally strong in the face of big challenges and believing with all of our being that there is a way forward – we just need to find it – is paramount to traversing the unknown, and was the difference between life and death in this case.

6. Don't give in to your fears

We are all just one decision away from success, but what keeps us stuck on the rock is the negative story that we tell ourselves. If I had talked myself into staying on the rock, and waited hopefully for someone to find me, there's a good chance I would have starved or frozen to death.

7. Get creative at problem-solving

Creativity and problem-solving are two of the most highly sought-after skills employers now look for, and for good reason. The ability to think outside the box in non-linear ways and piece together information in new and interesting combinations is what makes world-class leaders. Having a solutions-focused mindset is one of the best ways to approach decision-making and life in general. You will experience more success as a result, and see possibility where others see none. In some cases, the results may even be lifesaving. Thomas Edison, Henry Ford, Steve Jobs, Jeff Bezos all saw creative ways to navigate through the challenges they faced, whether that was adversity, dealing with naysayers or the fact that it hadn't been done before. They focused on what they could control – their own ability to keep problem-solving.

8. Faith matters

We must have faith in something greater, in a vision for the future to keep us going. It enables us to seek out opportunities and reprioritise our actions based on the new information we receive.

This experience taught me to have faith in myself, and to trust that the path exists. In order to get off the mountain safely, I needed to believe that it was possible in the first place. If I had entertained the thought that getting off the mountain was an impossibility, and started to tell myself that story, then I may well not have had the courage or strength to search out new options or even made it across the cliff face.

This whole experience showed me that in the most intense and hostile situations, it is possible to get increased clarity. This, combined with calmness, can lead to outstanding results.

I have learned to apply the lessons from this experience, and it has changed the way I approach the unknown and also my business. It is my hope that by sharing this story and the lessons I learnt, it will allow you to benefit in a similar way.

I trudged through the snow for another hour or so, relieved to be away from the cliff, but my mindset meant I would not stop until I found my way back to the main piste again. I clipped my board on one foot and scooted along the flatter snow. As the snowboarders among you will recognise, this is a technique for travelling across snow when the slope reaches a plateau. It was also a way for me to control the situation, should I find a hidden crevasse. One lucky escape was enough for one day. I should point out that I was still on high alert. I was acutely aware that even though the slope looked tame, I was still off-piste with no idea if I was going in the right direction.

My goal here was to get the job done as efficiently as possible, and it wasn't done yet. As much as the landscape was untouched and beautiful, I did not stop to admire it or take it in. This wasn't a sightseeing tour. This was a rescue mission. I was still all alone and I was the only one responsible for my survival, as had been the case for the last four hours or so. It was important to remember these points as the success of getting down the cliff, away from immediate danger could have clouded my judgement and caused me to get lost or make risky decisions.

I kept the pep talks up, speaking my decisions out loud at each fork in the road, trying to get my bearings as best I could. When you are up there in the mountains, it is easy to get disorientated.

After boarding across the wilderness for a while, I eventually found a ski slope and meandered calmly down. As if on autopilot, I got on the ski lift and went back up to the top of the mountain – despite the fact I was trying to go home. I don't know what came over me. I took the first lift back down to the chalet and let the enormity of what had just happened wash over me.

When I got back to the chalet, two of the guys were outside on the balcony smoking. I can't remember who they were exactly, but they looked like twins and they were part of the physiotherapy group. They had snuck out of the lectures early to hang out and drink a few beers.

They asked me how my day had been and I told them. Over the course of half an hour, I regaled the tale as they stood there silently listening in awe. I don't think it was until I actually spoke the words that I fully realised how close I had come to death. The look on their faces as they listened intently and asked questions made me accept what had happened.

I wandered off and went out to explore the night in the village of Verbier. I think it's something about being a teenager, perhaps you don't quite get it, or you do get it and you are able to move on, but it wasn't like I broke down in tears.

When I got back to the chalet for dinner, it was clear I was the talk of the evening. Everyone was waiting for me to tell them first-hand what had happened. Stevie couldn't really give two shits about my ordeal on the mountain. This directed attention away from him and his antics so it was wasted in his eyes, but those that got it got it and listened.

I gave my mum a big hug. She had obviously been told of my ordeal by the other people in the group. However, these guys were going too far, wanting to focus on the 'what if' or 'what could have gone wrong' aspects of the experience, not the miraculous tale of my fight for survival that I had told them earlier. Negative self-talk hadn't been a part of my strategy on the mountain and I wasn't about to start it now when retelling the story. I remember feeling indifferent to their requests for details. The fact that they were only interested in one thing, how close I came to dying only a few hours earlier, made it harder to convey the full experience.

If I was in their shoes, I would have probably done the same thing. Enthusiasm takes over, and you don't realise the person who's gone through the experience could offer you more value about what it was like on the mountain, the changes they went through, the thoughts and emotions experienced.

It may also have been because I didn't want to scare my mum. In a way, I thought I was protecting her by not engaging with the dramatic details that everyone else seemed keen on getting out of me. Or maybe, after coming moments from death and figuring my way down to safety, I just wasn't in the mood for the dramatics. It seemed childish, like they didn't get it, but how could they really? It hadn't been them up there alone on the mountain. They hadn't had to take responsibility and navigate a safe course to be here now, living.

My mum was just happy that I had made it back alive, she trusted me fully, and always had, but hearing the rumours of my near-death experience from the group probably wasn't the best for her. I guess looking back at it now with my 'adult brain', and as a father myself, it would have been a good idea to go find her and tell her what had happened straight away, rather than letting her find out from a group of entertainment-hungry scaremongers. But as a teenager who had just snatched his life back from the jaws of death, I needed to get back to reality, to move on, to go have some fun.

What happened to me had a profound effect on me, it changed me, gave me perspective, gratitude and clarity.

The experience had brought me closer to God and shown me my spiritual side that was sometimes hidden. It had also fortified my belief in my mental and physical ability to make decisions in extreme circumstances. I felt proud of my actions, but not in a boastful way, in a necessary way. I did what was necessary to complete the mission that was given to me.

Since that day, I haven't told many people about the experience until now. It was only when I realised that it had changed me and that sharing my experience could improve the decision-making abilities of others, that I decided to write it down and share my story.

Operating from this mission-driven mindset that I learned on the mountain has helped me in plenty of decision-making situations since then, both in business and my personal life. As a society, we are often told to be cautious when making a decision and to weigh up all the options. But sometimes (in fact, more often than not) we just don't have access to absolutely all the information before we need to make a decision. Being able to make decisions quickly and decisively is a skill that phenomenal business leaders possess. They are able to operate with just 50% of the information and move forward, accepting responsibility for the consequences.

If it helps you, remember that decision-making doesn't mean setting a fixed course of action and moving forward on autopilot regardless, it provides the option to pivot at any given stage. When new information presents itself, being able to pivot and have the courage to optimise your decision is a killer skill to acquire.

Making a decision allows you to get feedback from your environment more quickly than if you just sit and deliberate.

Decision-making and you

Now I want you to ask yourself, is there a big decision you have been putting off? A conversation you need to have?

Now is the time to rip off the band-aid and make the decision to go forward. To have the difficult conversation, to apply for the job of your dreams, to quit the job that's sucking your soul and draining your motivation.

This is your one time on this planet and the sooner you get into the habit of making quick and effective decisions, the more you'll have the opportunity to experience and fulfil who you are truly meant to be.

> **Your full potential is calling you and you won't reach it by staying stuck on the fence. It's out there, and once you start acting like the person you want to become, you'll step into those shoes and start living life on your terms.**

Effective decision-making should feel good. It should feel like a weight has been lifted and you can now focus on the execution. There is a mindset shift that needs to happen away from blame and fear. If you make a decision and take action that doesn't work out the way you planned, don't default to blaming or hating yourself. This can be easy to do, but part of taking responsibility for making the decision and carrying it out is taking responsibility for when things don't go as planned. When things don't go right, make sure you learn whatever valuable insights you can from the situation, so that you can apply them to future situations and move forward once again. Responsibility isn't just accepting the outcome, it's agreeing to use what is given and playing the game at a higher level, despite what happens to you.

Do you think that every great leader or entrepreneur got to where they are now by not making the wrong decision?

No. It's what they did with the information and the lessons they received when they got it wrong that made all the difference and allowed them to surpass everyone else.

They maintained a commitment to their vision, in spite of all the wrong turns. The wrong turns led them to the right turns, and so taking the wrong turn is part of the journey. If you can teach your mind to think in this way, rather than beating yourself up every time you make a wrong decision, you will beat the negative cycle of self-doubt and build a positive, self-empowering cycle that lifts you up and allows you to achieve great things in any given situation.

In a way, this near-death snowboarding experience was a gift, as I learned decision-making at the highest level, which gave me the ultimate advantage in life going forward. My wrong turn that day became a source of power because it taught me so much.

Being placed in those circumstances and playing the game of life with such high stakes forced me to learn in a highly pressurised, accelerated way. At the time, it didn't feel like I was learning, it felt like I was connected and experiencing life on a completely new level.

I found the sense of calm, cool-headedness hard to replicate at other points in life, but the experience showed me that it is there, it does exist, and I can draw upon it at times of intense challenge. It is a plane of living and a state of mind that enables you to exist calmly and execute life or death decisions time after time, even though the odds are heavily stacked against you.

> **Listen to your inner self. Don't take a tricky situation at face value, look beyond the veil instead. Pull back the curtain and see that there is more to it. Nothing is impossible and you have the know-how within you to produce amazing results that are far beyond what the world would have you believe.**

When we focus our energy in a positive way and direct it towards looking for opportunities, they are then drawn to us. Doors open as a result and pathways clear.

This trip was truly special to me. I didn't know it then, but surviving this ordeal would give me two more years with my mum on this Earth. In 2006, she very sadly contracted a devastatingly aggressive form of cancer which rapidly spread from her skin to her bones. Within weeks, it was categorised as stage 5 (the final stage) before we even had a chance to try and stop it. This was the hardest thing I have ever had to come to terms with, making decisions from this point onwards without Mum in my life was not something I had expected to undertake. But by having this winter trip together and learning to navigate an extreme situation on my own had, in some ways, prepared me to take on the responsibility of thinking for myself and taught me the power of effective decision-making.

My mum was an inspiration to me in many ways, not only because of her enthusiastic and positive manner, but also because of the passionate way she would go after things she believed in fully. When she had an idea or a spark of inspiration she wanted to get to it right away. She didn't want to wait; she was undeterred by naysayers and always drummed into me that anything is possible.

Losing Mum was one of the hardest things I have ever experienced. I wasn't prepared, ready or willing to accept her leaving this world, but having that last holiday with her, and going through that adventure gave me so many amazing memories that I still cherish to this day. It's not the way I would have liked it, but I do thank the guidance that was looking after me up on the mountain that day, as it enabled me to finish the trip with her alive and in one piece.

> **There is one piece of advice that Mum gave me which has changed the course of my life dramatically, and that is to courageously go after your big goals, dreams and passions.**

I have tried to step more fully into living this way, and I would encourage you to do the same.

I have learned through her example when I make decisions about what to do, especially when they seem to be risky. I have learned, through her example, that it is better to go for it and experience life in all its glory, rather than just sit on the sidelines and hope that you can get the same level of understanding, wisdom and knowledge.

We can only expand our horizons by partaking fully in life, and even if we do not achieve what we set out to accomplish, there is always a lesson worth discovering that life is willing to teach us if we try.

***

A month later, I decided to take action on my goal of working a ski season, so I travelled to Milton Keynes and applied for a managerial position in a hotel in Chamonix, France, that had just become available.

Some poor soul had broken his leg and was coming home. Within a week, I got offered the job and I was on my way to start my ski season in France, and boy what an adventure that was. But that story is for another time. I had come a long way from looking enviously at the cool snowboarders in the bar in Verbier and had effectively become one of their tribe. I had put my plan into action.

Now you have read my story and seen first-hand how I applied the principles of decision-making to an extreme situation, I want to outline these tools in more detail in the second part of this book.

PART 2

DECISION-MAKING TOOLS AND TECHNIQUES

CHAPTER 5

DECISION STRATEGY: MY GO-TO DECISION-MAKING MODELS

"Better a good decision quickly than the best decision too late."

— Harold Geneen

A KEY PART of decision-making is knowing *why* you are choosing to do something and weighing up the consequences. Effective decision-making requires doing this at speed and learning to calibrate for a shift in direction as new information presents itself.

Below, I'm going to run through the best decision-making models to enable you to not only become an efficient decision-maker and reduce the need for umming and ahhing, and procrastinating, so that you can take advantage of opportunities, but also increase the effectiveness of your decision-making. Efficiency is great, knowing how to make a decision at speed, but effectiveness is vital. This is about being able to adapt to new information and transform results. Once you know what your goal is, then you can really start to have some fun.

With each technique, I'll explain how it works, give you some ideas on when to use it and show you how you can start using it in practice. I'll then round off with some pros and cons (so you can understand when to deploy it). Hopefully, you'll get a feel for how each tool can help you make better decisions.

Let's turn you into a decision-making pro.

1. If/Then Decisions

How this works

This is a rules-based decision-making technique that works much like a mathematical formula. On the one side, there are inputs and on the other, there is an outcome. The outcome is determined by predefined rules that dictate how you will respond to what has just happened.

If/then decisions work like this – you decide in advance that you will respond if a certain thing happens. For example, if anyone cuts in front of you in a queue, you'll ask them what they are doing. Or if you see a homeless person, you will give them a dollar.

The beauty of this technique is it's quick, as it uses a pre-set response, leaving you mentally free from your duty to decide in the moment or on the fly.

This means that you'll make consistent decisions, rather than ad-hoc decisions, which could be influenced by all manner of factors ranging from your mood, to what you ate in the morning, to a bad night's sleep or just a whimsical change of heart.

When to use this

There are plenty of opportunities to use this at work. For example, if you're fed up with being paid late, then make a rule that if your pay cheque is deposited more than two days late into your bank account you'll escalate it to finance and push back. Or if your boss keeps cutting you off mid-sentence in meetings, make a rule that if he does it more than three times during a single interaction, you'll say something to him.

How to use this

By employing the if/then technique, you're free from having to decide what to do. You've already decided! Now you're ready to act like a boss. The next question is, how do you go about deciding what decisions you want to 'automate' with an if/then model. I suggest you use if/then decisions to deal with low-medium priority decisions, such as what to wear, what to eat, what you will do if your friend is late. As you build up confidence using this technique, you may branch out and get more adventurous. You can use this tool to push yourself to do uncomfortable, yet growth-producing things by setting yourself challenges. For example, if the speaker at a conference asks the audience for a volunteer, you decide that you'll put your hand up, or if the CEO asks if there are any questions at the next company all-hands meeting, you decide that you'll ask a question thereby pushing yourself into new territory.

Essentially, the skill of knowing when to use the if/then tool comes with practice, which will then form a habit. There are a multitude of circumstances where if/then decisions can help you from getting stuck on which way to turn. So, the next time you face a quandary, I challenge you to ask yourself, is this an appropriate time to bring out the if/then decision?

Pros

The best thing about this is it's a huge time saver – once the conditions are met, you already have a path pre-mapped out of what you are going to do, so actioning that will take up very little brain space compared to devising a new path every time.

Limitations

However, a cautionary note here. This only works well for predictable, simple, and known events. It would not be advisable to employ this approach when you are developing a new product or deciding which company to acquire, because of its linear nature you'd be shutting out a wealth of potentially advantageous options. In these situations, more strategic decision-making is required to seek out the right answer.

2. Habits

How this works

If/then decisions form the basis of what we call habits. Habits are actions performed consistently over time that create routines, which then become rituals if they are performed over a number of months as you go about your life. Our decisions define our habits which define our actions, and it is these actions that give us our deserved outcomes. Healthy habits enable you to make better decisions because once you have pre-set intentions, you will be able to follow the rules to make quick, high-quality decisions. Habits can eliminate the decision-making process entirely, leaving you free and energized to handle your business. An example of this is getting up early. You set your alarm for 5am and get up when it goes off, and start to complete the tasks you need to get done, e.g. work out, read, write, meditate, and make breakfast. As getting up early is a habit, there's no hitting the snooze button, or indecision, the task of getting out of bed is completed automatically. The decision is made.

It's why Barack Obama chose to wear similar clothes each day, to remove the burden of choice so that he would have one less thing to worry about and could attend to more pressing matters, like, I don't know, running the United States of America.

It's why Steve Jobs did much the same thing with his classic black turtleneck, jeans and sneakers, day in and day out. I mean, if defined habits, like eliminating the need to decide what you are going to wear in the morning, lead you to invent the iPhone or be President of the United States then I am all for it.

It's these small shifts in how you approach each day that build up and increase what you can actually get done in your day. This will enable you to spend more time on the things you want to and enable you to focus more. Put simply, consistent habits increase your ability to stick to a decision.

Our decisions define our habits, which define our actions, and it is these actions that give us our deserved outcomes. For instance, if you first decide on the type of person you want to become, you can use habits as a way to direct your progress. For example, you decide you want to be a healthy weight, which means losing 10 kilos. You decide to eat healthily and make it a habit, and therefore make different choices around what goes into your body. Decisions are not always easy, mind you, but the formation of habits can help to direct your progress down a certain path and make it easier to resist anything that could throw you off.

Having formed the habit of eating a salad at your work canteen every day (instead of the fried food you used to go for), and having done this for a couple of weeks, you won't even be tempted the next time they have a greasy fast-food option, because you will be deeply entrenched in your 'I have salad for lunch at work every day' habit. You will walk over to the salad bar, like you do every day, and start filling up your plate. Whereas, if you hadn't built the habit and just had salad sometimes, it would be much easier for you to get tempted by the greasy stuff.

As we go through life, we experience growth as we are exposed to new situations, cultures, challenges, hardships, lessons, and people. It, therefore, makes sense that some habits evolve as we grow and some habits never change, keeping us grounded and on course for success.

When to use this

Daily. By integrating decent habits into your normal daily life, you are able to stop yourself veering off course with bad decisions. You'll also save time and energy – as you won't even think about these decisions anymore.

How to use this

You need to create habits that are aligned with the life you want to live. For example, if you want to keep healthy, setting the habit to eat pizza every Friday, Saturday and Sunday is not great, whereas going for a run around your local park every Saturday morning is. So, take the time to make sure you set the right habits. The way to go about selecting habits that support your vision and goals is to look at people doing what you want to do or achieving the goals you want to achieve and then mirroring their actions. Ask yourself this question: What would I need to do to achieve that? Start by finding out what works for a range of high performers in the same area you want to achieve in, and then you can begin to test and learn what works for you. For example, if you want to start your own business whilst also being there for your family, what would you need to do to achieve this? For starters, from my own knowledge of what high performers do to get ahead is, you'll need to get up early whilst the family is sleeping. They work to develop their own businesses during this time so that they can be more present when the family is awake. They build networks of people on the same or similar paths, put their health and well-being high up on the list and balance both sets of responsibilities. Emulating and learning from other people in your life who are doing the thing you want to succeed in is one of the quickest and most effective ways of forming habits.

Habits allow you to make progress quickly in the realm of decision-making, enabling you to streamline your actions. They will provide the backbone to the attainment of your goals, as long as you remain aware of when they hold you back from achieving more, trying new things and extending your growth.

The next time you witness yourself making an automatic decision, ask yourself, am I doing this because I want to or because it's a habit and just what I always do? How is this habit benefiting me right now? How could I improve this habit if I had to? By focusing in on these questions you might be surprised by your answers. If so, it could be time for an upgrade in the habit department.

Pros

If you want to be the next big thing in the start-up scene, then you can't get caught up on deciding whether to wear the red or pink scarf or figuring out if you'll have dessert.

Make better choices around the small stuff and you'll have time to work on the problems that really matter, like finding an addressable market that is underserviced for your innovative new product.

Limitations

It may take a little time to set up the habit in the first place, but after that, it will become routine and you won't have to think about it at all. Yes, that's right, it will use up zero brain space.

Habits are sticky. What do I mean by this? They go largely unnoticed and if they are not checked regularly, they can lead you away from where you actually want to end up. For example, if you get a pang of hunger every night at 9pm and automatically (and unconsciously) reach to pour yourself a bowl of cereal, this will increase your sugar intake over time and lead you further away from your goal of getting slim. Habits like this can be hard to change once they are set. As much as habits provide us with the opportunity to stay consistent, we must ensure that we are consistent where it matters.

Take being busy, for example. If you check your phone 55 times throughout the day, in case you have a new email or someone wrote a comment on your Instagram page, you aren't being productive with your time. The key with habits is to reduce them to the ones that matter only and then eliminate the rest.

Take a stock analysis of how many habits are controlling your daily life and you might be surprised at how many you discover. This is a fantastic thing and awareness is the first step to taking back control. Once you become aware, make sure that you question whether the habit is taking you closer to your goals or further away and then conduct this practice once a month.

3. Time Limits

How this works

One decision strategy that works well when complete and utter standstill is likely is to make the best decision within a given timeframe.

In most cases, not doing anything at all is the worst decision you can make. It is better to make a decision than to fall into the bottomless pit of hopeless despair that is decision paralysis. This is not a place where you want to be as it causes people, businesses and institutions to miss out on all manner of opportunities for fear of making the wrong decision. I'll dive into this mysterious beast in more detail later.

Be warned, the illusion of doing nothing is just that, an illusion. The decision has been made and it leaves you fixed, rigid and frozen, on top not knowing what's the right path to go down.

So, give yourself a time limit to ensure you don't sit back and do nothing.

When to use this

Decisions will stagnate when:

1. There is no clear answer jumping out and all your options seem to have equal merit for different reasons and the impact of each option must be investigated in more detail. This is especially true of big decisions. However, in a worst-case scenario, this causes the decision-making process to fall into a spiral of indecision, where no clear decision can be agreed upon. This is especially common in complex situations that involve multiple factors and have a multitude of potential

outcomes, each of which needs careful consideration.

2. People have strongly held views and don't consider alternatives.
3. The stakes are so high that fear of making the wrong decision freezes the process.

If you use the time limit in any of these scenarios, you are forcing yourself to make the best decision, based on the information at hand at that time, and committing yourself to support that decision to move it forward.

How to use this

When you place time limits and deadlines on decisions, it is important to remain responsible for the quality of that decision. You need to become the ambassador for high standards, rather than using the deadline as an excuse to rush the decision-making process.

Another way to move the decision-making process forward is to place self-imposed deadlines on the outcome and not the decision itself. For example, an author writing a book might say, 'I will have this book finished by December 1st no matter what.' The deadline then acts as a device to trigger the question, 'In order to do that, what do I need to do?' which, in turn, provokes both the choices and decisions you need to make. Keeping this deadline in front of mind helps us to make the decision process easier because we are able to weigh up the pros and cons of taking certain actions in the moment. For example, should I go out to dinner with friends tonight or should I stay in and write the book? Should I relax by watching this awesome new movie that just came out or should I stay in and write the book? With the deadline imposed, making a decision around these daily life choices becomes simpler. It forces us to do the work and we begin to instinctively know and trust what the right decision is more frequently. That's not to say that sometimes taking a break and watching the awesome new movie starring Leonardo DiCaprio won't be the right choice. The lesson here is that by imposing deadlines, we consciously make a commitment to value the decisions we make more carefully, which helps to keep us to honour that deadline.

Pros

Being able to recognise when the decision-making process has stalled and then initiating deadlines and time limits enables us to regain momentum from all parties. It helps to stop us from overthinking decisions, which is the worst. Time limits and deadlines give us the opportunity to make the best decision with the information we have at the time. Remember, in any situation, you will never have all the information. By being decisive, making a decision, and moving forward with the plan, you will find out new information that you can use to pivot your decision later when you uncover crucial information. This is called progress.

Limitations

If time limits are overused, their effectiveness wears off and deadlines will get extended, missed or even ignored. Imagine using a time limit to make every decision. This might work on an individual basis, but as the number of people involved and the complexity of the situations increases, the time limit could become a hindrance rather than a saviour.

Another potential downfall is you could miss out on important details and decide against creative solutions because you fear they may take too long to explore or you don't have time to consider all the options.

The risk that comes with relying on deadlines to complete tasks and kick ass in the decision-making department is that you can come over as a cold uncaring machine-like person when dealing with other people. This is something for you to manage; high effectiveness comes from knowing yourself, what you need to be productive and how to influence others by using soft skills like empathy.

> **What we are aiming for here is a careful assessment of the information on hand and an effective decision that is made as a result of the process. The point isn't to make a fast decision just for the sake of it.**

The importance of remaining calm under pressure is a key skill when you have to make decisions in time-bound situations, whether these are self-imposed or otherwise. In a similar vein, you will excel by staying detached from the emotion of the situation and staying focused on producing high-quality decisions.

4. Find People Who Disagree With You

How this works

When you think you know the answer, it can be useful to seek others' opinions. In some way, the opinions of those who disagree with you are the most important as they may see things from a different perspective, which enables them to flag issues you can't see.

The concept of meritocracy is best demonstrated at Ray Dalio's hedge fund, Bridgewater. In his memoir *Principles: Life & Work* he says, *'Rather than thinking, "I'm right," I started to ask myself, "How do I know I'm right?"'*

Ray adopted this approach to thinking about everything that he and his employees did at Bridgewater. This pivot occurred after he predicted that the stock market would crash when, in fact, it went on one of the longest winning streaks in history.

As a result of this decision, and the confidence that he was right, Ray nearly had to shut up shop. After losing so much of his clients' money, he had to let go of all of his staff and even borrow four thousand dollars from his dad to help keep his family afloat. Not easy times, and difficult to stomach I am sure, especially if you bet the company and your reputation on the outcome.

These were challenging times for Ray, but the gift was in the lesson that he took from this humbling experience. Moving forward, he balanced his audacious approach to investing with a new-found humility he'd been gifted, which allowed his strategies and ideas to be stress-tested, disagreed with and pulled apart.

Ray was ready to begin again, to rebuild Bridgewater to where it sits now as the world's largest hedge fund. To do this, Ray surrounded himself with the smartest people who would challenge his ideas with brutal honesty. If they thought he was talking nonsense and making poor decisions, he wanted them to speak up and say so; in fact, he created an environment where it was the norm.

In this radical transparent meritocracy, people can say what they think with visibility into all conversations and meetings. This means that decisions can be rigorously stress-tested by the collective of the group.

When to use this

Much like Ray's story, this technique can be used when you feel overconfident, such as when you may have missed something or your ego is running wild because you are so sure you're right. After all, if you're that confident you're right, it won't matter if you let another expert have a crack at picking holes in your argument.

How to use this

A step back from this line of thinking would be to form The Mastermind Group, as discussed in Napoleon Hill's 20-year study *Think and Grow Rich*. The purpose of a mastermind group is to surround yourself with people that force you to step-up a level, grow and expand your perspectives. Divergent thinking collected from a mastermind group can be highly advantageous.

Go out into the world and find intelligent people who can stress-test your thinking. This is likely to be other experts or people who have similar interests, which doesn't mean your nearest and dearest family members.

Pros

It's like people go from seeing things in one dimension (their opinion) to all dimensions (all opinions). We can agree that if it is done well, collective decision-making can produce more outstanding results than individual decision-making.

If you get out there and consult with experts who will give you their opinion and stress-test your decision, thinking and rationale, you open up yourself and your ideas to integration, introspection and broaden the diversity of thinking that is involved with your plan. Taking this approach, you'll be privy to a host of objections, concerns, and counterarguments that you may not have considered.

This is valuable feedback and your plans may get torn to shreds, but withstanding this battery of assaults from experts in the field is better than making a mistake.

Finding people to disagree with you can also help you avoid future pitfalls so that you can do things differently, adjust and predict the future. This is because people who can predict the future are also able to create it with the mind.

Ray Dalio wrestled with this thought when he predicted the wrong timing of a market downturn in the 1980s. He asked himself, 'What would I do differently in the future so that I wouldn't make that mistake?' His answer was the idea meritocracy. In essence, finding clever people who have different opinions to you and getting them to challenge your ideas and pick holes in them, so that you can really see how robust they are.

Limitations

It doesn't come without criticism. Being honest and allowing for that level of honesty to exist comes with a host of negative objections, anywhere from lacking empathy to a 'brutal working environment'. If you ask for brutally honest opinions, you have to be prepared to handle them. Dalio says, 'We've found that 25-30% of the population it's just not for,' but he argues, 'collective decision-making is much better than individual decision-making if it's done well, it's been the secret sauce behind our success, it's why we've made money 23 out of the last 26 years.'

The challenge with this is dropping your ego; gaining a thicker skin and putting your ideas out there isn't for everyone. The other challenge is who you surround yourself with. It can't just be anyone, it needs to be people with an expertise in the topic of discussion.

5. Six Thinking Hats Technique

How this works

Edward de Bono's Six Thinking Hats is a powerful tool to help you look at problems from different perspectives by helping your thinking to become organised and improved. The idea behind it is that collaboration is good – great, in fact. But there is a myth at work here. The typical idea of teamwork is that all the members are harmoniously on the same page, working together in sync, digging in and working effectively together without the presence of conflict.

As we've already discovered, conflict and disagreement are elements that are required for effective decision-making because they force you to address multiple vantage points and consider otherwise ignored information.

Each hat is a different colour and shape to represent a different frame of thought. The purpose is to force you to look at the problem from multiple perspectives. This allows you to uncover new insights and reduce the effect that single-mindedness can have on your decision. In effect, it allows you to fully unpack the issues or problems being discussed, giving you a more holistic and robust picture.

The purpose is to enable you to think deeply about a topic and reduce the influence of previously held prejudices that could interfere with your decision-making process. It is supposed to shake things up and allow new frames of reference to enter the conversation, including additional points of view to be heard and different narratives to be considered. It's pretty epic really, because if you think about it, when do we actually stop and get some structure about how we think what we think? Normally, we just go along with our daily lives, inputting our thoughts and regurgitating them when required without consciously sitting down and analysing where they came from and what other frames of reference it could be valuable to consider. De Bono was on to something when he developed this bad boy, I tell you.

Edward de Bono's[1] six hats are:

White Hat – INFORMATION

[1] Mulder, P. (2011) *Six Thinking Hats*. Retrieved (2019) From ToolHero. http://www.toolhero.com/decision-making-six-thinking-hats-de-bono

Considers only the information, facts and figures available.

Red Hat – EMOTIONS

Only gives an intuitive emotional perspective involving feelings when looking at the problem.

Black Hat – JUDGEMENT

Plays 'devil's advocate' by identifying barriers and mistakes.

Yellow Hat – POSITIVE

Looks for opportunities; takes a positive, harmonising view.

Green Hat – CREATIVITY

Provokes, nurtures and investigates. Gives ideas space to evolve and hears what they are about.

Blue Hat – THINKING/ORGANISING

Thinks about the thinking that needs to be done, how it will be carried out and what happens next. You are like the facilitator.

The six hats tool works best when you are in a team and trying to decide on the best course of action, although you can also use it on your own (although it might look a bit weird if you're sat in your office, putting on different hats and having a conversation with yourself).

When to use this

Use the six hats when you want to look amazing in front of your boss. It's perfect for when there is absolutely no progress being made and the group decision-making process seems to be idling somewhere between nowhere and, 'Is this conversation still happening? Kill me now.' I find six hats is most effective when you are either decision-making in groups, or making big complex mammoth-sized decisions with multiple parts to consider.

Here's a quote from the man himself: 'Creativity involves breaking out of established patterns in order to look at things in a different way.'[2] I couldn't have said it better myself. So there you have it, break the patterns people and let's get creative.

How to use this

If you're anything like me and want to have a little fun, I would recommend dressing up for the occasion and using actual hats or, if you're pushed for time, metaphorical hats that indicate a change in the frame of thinking.

---

[2] https://www.toolshero.com/decision-making/six-thinking-hats-de-bono/

If you're on your own, then the best way to use this instrument is to spend 2-5 minutes taking on the role of each hat. Jot down or speak out loud the key arguments and perspectives for each of the six different themes (Pro tip – record the session on your phone for later reference, seeing as there is only you to recall the information). Once you've finished, you should have identified a number of different, valuable points for consideration; the idea being that you are now in a better position to make a more well-rounded decision about the best route forward.

If you are rolling this out to a team, I would encourage you to start by explaining *why* you are doing this exercise. Give the crowd a little context before whipping out your magical hats as you risk looking like some kind of hat sorter from Harry Potter's Hogwarts. People aren't always going to agree with new tools or methodologies, especially at times of increased pressure, so you've got to sell it to them. This is majorly important when the decision is a high-risk high-reward type and there's a lot at stake. It is much easier to slip this kind of thing in earlier so that different stakeholders in the business get used to it and can see the success stories for themselves before you walk into the boardroom and pour a load of de Bono on the situation, wanting to save the day.

To take this one step further – as I always like to give you the absolute maximum – the six hats can be reorganised into combinations so that the thinking can be directed towards a specific goal.

Below are some awesome ways you can cut this to achieve certain goals.[3] For example, if you wanted to gather feedback on an idea really fast, you'd go blue hat, black hat, green hat, white hat, blue hat, or in other words *thinking, judgement, creativity, information, thinking.* I say, do whatever works best for you. If the list below is of value to you, use it and check out toolhero.com for more details.

Goal	Hat Sequence
Initial Ideas	Blue, White, Green, Blue
Choosing Between Alternatives	Blue, White, Green, Yellow, Black, Red, Blue
Identification of Solutions	Blue, White, Black, Green, Blue
Fast Feedback	Blue, Black, Green, White, Blue
Strategic Planning	Blue, Yellow, Black, White, Blue
Process Improvement	Blue, White, Yellow, Black, Green, Red, Blue
Problem-solving	Blue, White, Green, Red, Yellow, Black, Blue
Performance Assessment	Blue, Red, White, Yellow, Black, Green, Blue

Notice that all the sequences begin and end with the blue hat. This is because the blue hat brings discipline and focus to the process. It is like the coach and it's

---

[3] Mulder, P. (2011) *Six Thinking Hats.* Retrieved (2019) From ToolHero. http://www.toolhero.com/decision-making-six-thinking-hats-de-bono

the blue hat's job to think about thinking. The blue hat decides how the thinking will be done and then facilitates the exercise, deciding the order of the hats and finally reviews the outcomes and the next steps. Blue hat is like Coach K (for those of you who don't follow basketball, Ken Carter was a legendary coach of a team of underperforming students at Richmond High School in the USA, and took both their grades and ball-playing abilities to the next level).

Pros

It enables you to view the problem or decision from six different angles, taking in six very different, contrasting frames of thought. Sometimes we can easily become wedded to one particular frame of thinking without fully taking the time to consider any alternative ways of thinking about a problem.

Limitations

It's not always practical to roll out the six thinking hats. You might not have six people for a start to play each of the six hats, I certainly didn't when I was stuck on the side of the cliff.

If you conduct it yourself, then you may still be biased. Six hats is more time consuming than other techniques and it isn't the best to use in scenarios where time is a factor. For example, if a gigantic avalanche suddenly came thundering towards me, it wouldn't be the best way to handle decision-making. Can you imagine it: 'Ummm, hold on a minute, where's my blue hat?' Nope, it's not going to happen. So, time is a limitation with this one; when you need to make decisions fast this probably isn't your go-to.

That said, it has value and if you can get used to conducting the six hats approach at speed (e.g. 15 seconds per hat), it could enable you to make higher quality decisions because you will have a more rounded sense of the problem and the potential solutions available.

6. Warren Buffett's Two List Strategy

How this works

This strategy works well when you are attempting to organise a to-do list, your bigger life goals and objectives or you aren't sure where to focus your time to achieve optimal, fulfilling outcomes.

Start with a sheet of paper. Get it out now, we can do this one together. Begin by writing out your top 25 life goals that you want to achieve on the sheet. For instance, this could be milestones and victories, such as reaching financial independence before age 37, getting married, owning a house, going to Aruba, meeting Michelle Obama, or any one of the wondrous things you might have set your heart's desire on.

Remember, there has to be 25 items on your list before you can move on to the next stage so make them as juicy as possible. Don't worry about if you think they're obtainable right now, just focus on making them something you really want. The items on your list should make you salivate with anticipation. These are things you go to bed dreaming about; they are your top 25 life goals, after all!

Next, I want you to rank them in order of preference. If you could make them a reality, which one do you want most, then which is second, third, and so on.

Now get out a fresh sheet of paper and write preferences 1 to 5 on it. Call this sheet list A. Once you've done, grab another sheet and write items 6 through to 25 down. Call this sheet list B.

There's a reason why uber-successful people achieve their goals, it comes down to this simple strategy. Rather than spend your time trying to excel in all areas, you reduce the number of targets and focus all your time and energy on obtaining these few instead.

List A now becomes your Target List. List B becomes your Ignore At All Costs List. This strategy is a tool for clear prioritisation and focus.

When to use this

This tool is incredible for when you need to get focused on your strategy. This is a macro lens, big-picture thinking tool that can take a large set of data (25 items) and give you clear direction at the end of it. Warren Buffett is known for his sage advice and I would recommend using this tool for incredibly important matters, like planning your life goals, as in the example given above, or it could be used for your yearly plan, monthly plan, or any situation where you have a number of different objectives and you need to streamline your attention to get the most important ticked off above all else. I also use this tool when setting the vision for what I want to achieve within the week.

How to use this

It's a great tool if you find yourself overwhelmed and stressed out. If you are experiencing this right now, ask yourself, 'What is the most important thing I can do with my time right now?' and then do the 2-list exercise. You will feel like you have made progress because the route forward is becoming clear and you now have a road map for success.

Pros

It enables you to cut through your noise and simplify your goals to a handful of meaningful, purpose-infused desires that you have identified as your top life goals.

Limitations

Now comes the tricky part. In order for this to work, you must focus religiously on list A items until they are all completed. You must do this without getting distracted or diverted and you must not give any attention to items on list B.

Keep both lists with you and refer to them regularly. Take action consistently around list A items and ignore list B. The ability to consistently direct your focus towards the list A goals, without changing the objective, will enable you to reach them.

Summary

In summary, when it comes to decision-making there are plenty of tools that can help you to make a more accurate assessment from different perspectives, and then design a plan to achieve your desired results. However, amid all the noise and clutter it can be hard to know which tools are the best to use. Therefore, my intention for guiding you through this hyper-focused list of just six tools is that you will have a few up your sleeve to test out when you next struggle with which way to turn.

Now that you understand these six models for effective decision-making, I am going to show you how to avoid the most common pitfalls that occur. Keep going, you're doing awesomely!

CHAPTER 6

TOP 3 DECISION-MAKING PITFALLS TO AVOID

"Whenever you see a successful business,
someone once made a courageous decision."

— Peter F. Drucker

D ECISION-MAKING IS ONE of the most highly valued skills you can master today. It's what CEOs are paid the big bucks for. It's why entrepreneurs launching products go from zero to being practically everywhere in record-breaking time. The decisions we make matter and can transform the quality of our lives and how we experience the world around us. It's important to remember that we live not only in times of infinite opportunity and abundance, but also of great distraction. The overload of information coming at us across all channels 24/7 means there is a common tendency to mistake being busy, keeping up to date and responding instantly with being effective.

> **In decision-making, knowing what to focus on and what to stay away from (or ignore completely) is incredibly helpful.**

With the tools and lessons you have discovered so far in this book, you will fare pretty well when it comes to making your next important decision. However, there are three pitfalls that you absolutely need to watch out for, as these suckers will destroy your progress and momentum, and keep you fixated on the wrong details. Frustratingly, they can increase your stress at the exact moment when you need to remain calm, and will have you going around in circles, wreaking havoc in the most damaging ways if you don't pay attention to them. So, it's important you understand how to mitigate their influence when they appear.

In this powerful chapter, I will expose them, warn you when they will occur, and educate you on the techniques needed to overcome them. Fear not, we will come out the other side unscathed and you, my friend, will become one step closer to achieving mastery in the art of decision-making.

1. Decision Paralysis

What is decision paralysis?

Like a rampant beast that rears its ugly head the moment we have a big decision to make, decision paralysis tends to show up just when we least want it to and proceeds to suffocate and cloud our judgement. It's like it knows and has been waiting in the dark, lying dormant for this very moment to launch a surprise attack. It prevents us from choosing a course of action and moving on.

If you've experienced this yourself, I know how you feel; I'm right there with you. It is annoying and frustrating when this complete and utter 'opportunity blocker' shows up to the party uninvited, without a gift, and then sticks around, festering in the corner like a dirty mop.

Decision paralysis, if left unchecked, has the potential to hold you back in everything, and I mean everything – your career development, relationships and personal growth. Learning how to quickly distinguish when decision paralysis has taken hold and swiftly dealing with it, so you can get on with whatever you need to, is key to becoming an effective leader and master of your own life.

> "It is much more important that you are a good designer/manager of your life than a good worker in it."
>
> – Ray Dalio

When does decision paralysis strike?

You've probably noticed that it always seems to show up when a decision matters most. This is no coincidence. In fact, when we humans are presented with things that matter – job opportunities, important meetings, pitches, travel opportunities, scholarships – we tend to get stuck (if we're not careful).

Decision paralysis shows up in multiple forms but is predominantly and most commonly the over-analysis of our circumstances to the point that we fear the outcome and the process, or become so overwhelmed that we just stop dead in our tracks.

These are the most common occurrences:

1. **When something is really important**, we over-analyse or over-think because the stakes are high and we want to get it right. For example, deciding where to attend university or which house and area to live in. When it matters and there are a number of suitable options available, decision paralysis is often not far behind.

2. **When we are fearful of the consequences** and believe that our decision could potentially create a larger problem. For example, when you're sitting on a train and you notice you've lost your ticket. Informing the ticket collector of your mistake might result in you paying a fine, as it looks like you snuck onboard without a ticket, but not telling the ticket collector could lead to problems when you get off the train. In both situations, you fear the consequences and what larger problems your decision could create.

3. **When we think that the problem is too complex to solve**. An example would be a relationship where addressing an issue leads to the uncovering of multiple issues, making the already complex situation even more challenging.

4. **When there is too much choice available**. The overwhelm of choice, termed *overchoice* or *choice overload*, can ground down even the savviest business professionals. The more choices there are, the more likely you will experience regret or dissatisfaction over your decision. The reason for this is simple, cognitive dissonance occurs between the choice you have made and the perceived choice you *should* have made. The more options there are, the more cognitive dissonance you experience because the chances that you made the wrong decision are increased by virtue of there being more options on the table. I know, crazy, right? Who thought more options were a bad thing! For example, you saved up $5,000 to go on holiday but you have trouble deciding on where to stay because you're afraid that as soon as you book a better promotional offer or deal will come up. Does this sound familiar? I can certainly relate to it. In effect, you are stuck in decision paralysis because you fear that a superior solution is right around the corner. This is more common than you'd

imagine and crops up with all manner of golden opportunities.

5. **When we are terrified of making the wrong decision**. For example, when the stock market is rallying, but you are down to your last $1,000; everyone's telling you to jump in and invest but you just can't bring yourself to do it for fear of making the wrong decision. The fear of losing your last $1,000 is greater than the perceived rewards for taking action. So, what do you do? You do nothing, watching the market continue upwards, secretly hoping that it tanks and you can tell yourself that your fear was, in fact, sound judgement and responsible action – anything but fear. In this example, you don't invest because you are more afraid of losing the $1,000 than any potential returns you might get.

6. **When we don't have enough time**. Time is also a factor. When you are given a large set of options but only a short timeframe to make a decision, regret is often not far behind. If, however, you are given a longer timeframe to decide, the time pressure is dissolved, excitement starts to bubble and you can really weigh up the options by merit. This can be found in something as simple as deciding where to take an important client for lunch in a couple of days' time. As the minutes tick by, the date in the diary keeps creeping closer and

the feeling of not wanting to disappoint the client leads us to put off making a decision. Instead, we fall into decision paralysis. This, of course, continues until the pressure becomes unbearable and we wait until the last possible moment to decide. For some, this might resonate; 'What's the issue with this?' you might ask. The problem of living in this way is it's an extra burden to carry and this will weigh you down. By contrast, the proactive ass-kicker recognises time is short and jumps right to it, and by taking this course of action, they take ownership of their decisions, which is an empowering way to live.

There are just a few ways that decision paralysis crops up. Overall avoidance keeps you stuck in the minutiae, trapping you by bombarding your life with little stuff that hasn't been dealt with yet. This keeps you tied to the hamster wheel of life. It's not a deeply fulfilling way to live. Dealing with decision paralysis head-on helps you to feel more confident and enables you to elevate yourself to new levels of success. You'll feel free and more capable as a result. Next, I am going to offer you a crash course on how to rid yourself of this parasite once and for all.

How can you beat decision paralysis?

When life grips us in this way and we aren't sure which way to turn, it can be helpful to step back a little. When you are overanalysing, you're caught up in the whirlwind. It has you in its pull and can throw you about like a rag doll. You're too close and it can be hard to make sense of what's going on. Reactionary approaches are often misled with the best intentions, you analyse because you don't want to screw up, but in reality, that's exactly what ends up happening because you can't see the bigger picture.

To stop this ugly monster from taking hold when you notice yourself getting panicky or feel that your normal decision-making abilities start to disintegrate here are 5 steps to take.

5 Steps to deal with decision paralysis

1. **Commit to making a decision** – make a plan of attack for making a decision and call it your battle plan. In it, you define the rules that you'll play when making the decision, including the amount of time, money and resources you will dedicate to it and the amount of information you will consume. Then stick to it. Rigorously. Having a structured plan will help you to become less reactionary, emotionally reckless and more pragmatic.

2. **Step back from the situation** (a little) – zooming back out gives us perspective and allows our view of our world to expand. From this vantage point, we can see when we are being too much of a perfectionist or expecting too much from a

situation. It's important that you keep in mind that there are going to be bumps in the road, that's life. Having a big-picture view can allow you to see how this one decision isn't perhaps such a big deal in the grand scheme of things, how it is inevitable, or how it could enhance the attractiveness of your choices. Effective decision-making is preferable to waiting until it's too late and letting the decision be made for you, plus no one likes being trapped in a whirlwind of indecision. Taking a distanced, objective view will also help you to put things in perspective. Perhaps the outcome you imagine isn't justified, perhaps it is, but when you are caught up in the action, with a front-row seat, up close and way too personal to the situation at hand, it is only going to lead to one thing: paralysis.

3. **Ask yourself what you really want** – defining your priorities and objectives is a simple technique for cutting through the options, reducing the potential for over-analysis and setting out clear actions to follow. Take a leaf out of the Design Thinking (DT) methodology and make decisions in iterative steps. This is a process for creative problem-solving. You go through five stages in DT, which are, Empathise, Define, Ideate, Prototype and Test. I won't go through them all in detail, but taking the decision-making process in steps unburdens you from the pressure of getting too caught up

in the complexity of the whole. In the first two stages of Design Thinking, it is necessary to 1. develop a deep understanding of the problem (Empathise) and 2. clearly identify the problem you are looking to solve (Define). It is the same with asking yourself what you really want. The point is, to reduce the likelihood of decision paralysis, it is critical to get clear on what outcome you want to achieve.

4. **Stop thinking in binary terms** – when faced with a decision, it's easy to think in terms of 'yes or no', 'this or that', 'I do or I don't', 'I'm in or I'm out', without realising the options available rarely reflect such fixed terms. Decision-making doesn't have to be framed in this way. No one has put a gun to your head and given you an ultimatum. In reality, there are plenty more choices available to you. The next time you find yourself dealing with an outcome you perceive to be fixed, try to bring in a third option. By doing this you will allow adaption to enter the arena. Remember that decision-making is a flexible process and the combination of elements that make up the thing you are deciding on (e.g. event, outcome, product, service, location) can be rejigged, reordered and reworked at a moment's notice, by you. By its very nature, decision-making is an iterative process. As new information presents itself, new situational changes occur, like market dynamics that shift, relationships

that evolve, economies that rise and fall. The decisions you make need to be adaptable enough to move with the times.

5. **'Perfect is the enemy of the good.'** – Voltaire. Nothing is perfect. What is perfect anyway? Things can always be improved, but if you become hoodwinked into believing that a thing must not be decided upon or actioned until it is perfect, then you'll be waiting forever and a day to make it happen. Perfectionism can blur your view of reality. It has caused the cardiac arrest of many a beating heart in the dreams of would-be business owners, entrepreneurs, authors, musicians, and developers – the list is endless. Perfectionism is a killer of dreams. Those who wait, who fail to take responsibility for making a decision and committing to that process are ultimately risking failure by, ironically, not taking the necessary action due to their underlying aspiration of not wanting to fail. When faced with a decision, go with good; get your brilliance out into the world and let it shine. A short but powerful quote from Winston Churchill illustrates this point. After learning that the designers of World War Two landing craft were spending most of their precious time stuck in conflict over small tweaks to the design, he remarked, 'The maxim, "Nothing avails but perfection" may be spelt shorter. "Paralysis".'

2. Biases

What is it?

Yes, you are biased. You may not think it, or like what I am saying, but the truth of the matter is we all carry around our biases and impose them, even when we think that we're being impartial, objective and rational. In reality, we're jaded, skewed and prone to making illogical choices.

The concept of psychological bias was first introduced by psychologists Daniel Kahneman and Amos Tversky in a 1974 research paper titled, *'Judgement Under Uncertainty'*. It gained worldwide notoriety as it challenged the widely held notion that humans are rational creatures. Over the course of the next eight years, the pair set about researching all manner of human biases, such as the following:

Psychological or cognitive biases (as they're also called) creep into our decision-making process as if by magic. They affect the way we interpret data, read situations, and even how we view other people.

One example is confirmation bias. This means we see what we want to see, or rather we unconsciously give more preference, creditability or weight to a specific piece of information, behaviour or data set that happens to support our existing beliefs.

By definition, this means you choose to selectively ignore any information that goes against your beliefs. This is a problem!

When we can't be trusted to objectively factor in and take stock of all the relevant information that is available to us, it leaves us open to manipulation by, you guessed it, ourselves. Arrgh! How sneaky!

When does bias strike?

Bias can show up any time we make a choice or give an opinion by selectively ignoring information, either through unconsciously suppressing it or choosing to interpret the data in a favourable way. Much like the way that statistics can be spun to support any argument, information that is selectively interrupted can lead us down the garden path too.

3 Steps to deal with biases

1. Know when you are at the mercy of emotional biases. Be aware of them and do something to prevent yourself from being steered off track by them. The most common symptoms which can drive emotional biases are when you're feeling hungry, angry, lonely and tired (HALT). The HALT principle is to stop what you are doing and deal with the immediate issue before making any decisions. By learning the check for HALT when you are at a

decision-making crossroads you are becoming an effective decision-maker. Of course, this requires raising your self-awareness and taking simple steps to fix it. For example, if you're hungry, it is likely your stomach will growl, you may feel weaker physically or have trouble concentrating. These are all ways your body is telling you to nourish yourself. In the hectic chaos of meetings, presentations, commitments, we can forget that these warning signs mean something, and we push on through, forgetting that we aren't helping ourselves when it comes to making better decisions.

If you are angry, go to the gym and blow off steam rather than trying to solve the problem in front of you. As hard as it seems to stop and take a step back when we are highly emotional, we often make it worse by making a bad decision. You get the idea; the hard part isn't taking the action to alleviate the symptoms of HALT, it's having the self-awareness to recognise it in the first place and then having the self-control to do something about it. Obviously, in some situations making decisions when feeling any of the above is unavoidable, but where possible, you should try to increase your awareness of it and recognise its ability to throw you off your decision-making game (before it's too late), so you can resolve it and decrease the impact it has.

2. Educate yourself on the potential cognitive biases that may be at play in your life. A couple of hours spent learning about the possible biases and how that can infiltrate your daily life is time well spent. Tip – read *Thinking Fast and Slow* by Daniel Kahneman. Just briefly the ones you want to watch out for are:

   a. Recency effect (giving preferential treatment to the last piece of information, data or person you had contact with)

   b. Primacy effect (the same as recency, but this time you show a preference for the first information you received)

   c. Ambiguity bias (favouring choices with a known outcome versus taking a risk with unknown outcomes)

3. Availability

What is it?

This is another form of bias, but I have set it aside from the rest because I feel it is running rampant and causing havoc, so I want to address it here. Availability is where you make judgements and estimations based on how easily the data comes to mind. You let prevalence in your mind take precedence in your estimations and decision-making process.

For example, if there has been news of a terrorist attack in your capital city recently and you have been inundated with data, personal eye witness accounts and news reports on it, you might overestimate the likelihood of an attack occurring again due to the availability of information there is and the ease at which you can recall it, despite the fact that statistically, the chances of a terror attack in your capital city are very low.

In contrast, you might underestimate the devastating effect of a more common but mundane killer, like heart attacks, because you are less able to access significant information about this particular disease in your mind.

When does availability strike?

The media do this all the time to bolster their viewing numbers via clickbait headlines that sprout facts and figures, sensationalise certain eventualities and outcomes over others, and cause us to have a distorted view of the truth. Everyone knows about the danger of fake news.

3 Steps to deal with availability

The availability of reference points and how easily they can be made becomes your guide for judgement and estimation. When making decisions it is best practice to question what informational exposure could be influencing the confidence you have in your estimation.

1. **Ask yourself questions:** challenge yourself. Am I being overconfident? What don't I know? By stopping to take stock of a situation rather than just regurgitating what you have heard, you are purposefully injecting consideration into your decision-making process, thus making your research and analysis of the information more rigorous. Get into the habit of questioning your own assumption and try to ascertain how it is you know what you know. By recalling the source of the information and cross-checking its relatability, you will give yourself a tool to deal with overconfidence, remain humble and avoid some costly mistakes.

2. **Burst the bubble:** we live in a bubble. Each of us is constantly bombarded with adverts, opinions, all trying to influence our actions and gain an increased share of our greatest asset, our attention. The attention economy has arrived and it plays on availability bias for domination. To reduce this, create a high standard learning environment. By this I mean seek out and receive new, contrasting information from various sources. Allow yourself to be educated and listen to other viewpoints that may go against the grain of

society. You may decide you don't agree with them, you don't have to, but this high-quality synthesis of the information during decision-making keeps you stress-testing so-called facts so that you can reach more validated conclusions.

3. **Engage a mastermind group:** a diverse set of opinions and viewpoints comes in handy to counter the possibility of availability bias. It enables you to hear the other sides of the argument and protects you from making mistakes due to your ego.

Summary

The art of decision-making comes down to avoiding these pitfalls at all costs. The key to successfully keeping them at bay is to remain vigilant to the type of situations where it is likely they will crop up. The next step is to become hyper-aware of your own tendencies towards one or all of these decision-making pitfalls.

Whilst reading the last chapter, you may have actually acknowledged that you are guilty of falling into one of these traps. That's not a bad thing, now you have the opportunity to address them before they reappear.

The key to avoiding these traps is not to rest on your laurels. Even expert decision-makers can be thrown a curveball every now and again. Practise the steps outlined above when you notice that one of the three pitfalls has started to take hold. By doing so, you will diffuse its power and experience what psychologists call experiential learning.

In the final part of the book, I am going to reveal how masters of decision-making operate and the crucial thing they take control of to calmly handle any situation thrown their way.

PART 3

DECISION-MAKING MINDSET

CHAPTER 7

MENTAL FORTITUDE: HOW TO FEEL STRONG WHEN MAKING DECISIONS

"The price of greatness is responsibility."

— Winston Churchill

MENTAL FORTITUDE OR mental toughness is much like a muscle. The more you train your mind to bend to your will, the more control you have over how you perceive and interpret the world to be.

In this chapter, I'm going to teach you how to tap into a mentally tough mindset to become stronger. We will explore tools like reframing the situation, becoming stoic and finally acceptance. I will explain how each of these tools can help you make great decisions even in the most chaotic of situations.

1. Reframe

First, I'll also show you (via Simon Sinek) how to use the science of adrenaline to your advantage. This is a powerful technique, especially in high pressure, unknown and anxiety-inducing situations. This is one of the most practical, easy to implement and effective tools out there, so it's time to listen up. (If you've been reading along half-paying attention, half-chatting to your significant other in the kitchen, this is your wake-up call.)

In a moving speech given to a group of young students at Oliver Scholars[4], Simon Sinek, the world-famous motivational speaker, offered up a big penny drop moment for him, which he'd found in the world of professional runners. He explained how they trained themselves to interpret anxiety moments before a big race. He noticed that every time a reporter would interview an athlete after the race, they would ask the same question: 'Were you nervous?' and the athlete would respond, 'No, I was excited.' This response got Simon thinking deeply about the characteristics of anxiety and the similarity between the physical expression of what it's like to feel anxious and excited. In a nutshell, he concluded it is the same.

For example, when you feel really anxious, your palms get sweaty, your heart starts pounding faster, like it might pop out of your chest, and this is the exact same response when you are excited. The only difference between the two is the story that you tell yourself about what this physiological response means. On one hand, the story is you feel nervous and you really want it to stop. On the other, you are completely stoked, over the moon and delighted,

---

[4] Simon Sinek – Things I wish I knew when I was younger. 2018.
https://www.youtube.com/watch?v=p9gzGmyDJvc

overflowing with enthusiasm and charisma, the world is your oyster and the experience is insanely positive.

Therefore, at times of increased stress, surprise and danger, we can learn to reframe the story we tell ourselves about *what* these physiological signals mean and, in doing so, reduce our anxiety levels. How funny is that? All this time, the only difference between feeling anxious or excited is the story. You can start to see how the mind controls so much of what we experience, and if we can learn to control it, we can be more present and apply ourselves to the situation at hand to perform at our best. Magic! I was pretty pumped to find this out, and I am sure if you've got this far in the book then you are too. Thanks, Simon, for the helping hand.

Now I want to build on this theme of reframing and developing your perspective. How you interpret things, events and what happens to you, and the story you tell yourself can dramatically impact how you feel. Tell yourself a fearful story and you'll feel scared. Tell yourself a happy positive story and you'll feel radiant. Think of the difference between, 'I'm dreading this interview, that guy looks intimidating' and 'I'm really looking forward to this interview, this is my time to shine, whatever happens, I'll have fun and do my best.'

How to reframe

When you are worried or fearful of something, whether it is a future event, situation or circumstance, conduct the following exercise to develop a more positive frame of mind and regain a sense of optimism and control.

1. Start by describing your doubt or fear out loud.

2. Take out a piece of paper and draw three boxes. Label box one, 'best-case scenario', box two 'likely-case scenario' and box three 'worst-case scenario'.

3. Then, as best you can, try to imagine what each of these outcomes would be and describe it in each of the boxes.

By separating out and breaking down your fear, you can start to see there are alternatives to the worst-case scenario, and this act in itself will promote increased feelings of hopefulness and positive thinking. When we are fearful, we tend to only focus on the most extreme worst-case scenario, rather than the multitude of other outcomes that would be infinitely better and possible than where the mind is currently dwelling.

This exercise can be practised in many different fields. It could be used in sales, business, to conquer a fear of flying, weigh up moving countries, the principles remain the same. By breaking down and getting more diverse, positive perspectives, we disarm our fears and doubts of their power.

2. Be more stoic

Many people have been helped by Stoicism, which is based on the idea that even though you may not control external events, you can control how you respond to them. Stoicism offers a practical roadmap for making decisions and a direction for living that can be regarded as a philosophy of life.

Stoicism has benefits. It is associated with helping you to reduce panic in the midst of a crisis and gain control over your emotions so that you notice the opportunity contained within the setback and have the strength to forge a path through it.

To give you a little more flavour of the practice of Stoicism, I want to clear up a couple of misconceptions and describe its goal. In *A Guide To The Good Life: The ancient art of stoic joy,* William B. Irvine states that 'The stoics, as we have seen, thought tranquillity was worth pursuing, and the tranquillity they sought… is a psychological state in which we experience few negative emotions such as anxiety, grief and fear but an abundance of positive emotions especially joy.'

Misconception number 1: Stoics are grumpy, sad, pessimists that show no emotion. This is incorrect. Stoicism is different to 'being stoic', as it is described in a dictionary. When you are a practising Stoic you aren't suppressing all your emotions, bottling them up and never letting anyone know how you truly feel.

Instead, by practising Stoicism, you are just learning how to respond wisely to negative emotions.

For example, when faced with a really annoying situation, such as a man rudely jumping on the train while you try to get off and barging past you without any care for your safety. In this hypothetical but fairly common scenario, it would be normal to stop and say something to the ignoramus who has just abused your right of way. You won't let him get away with this. The outrage! So, what do you do? You chase after him and bellow a loud 'excuse me' to the carriage. Heads turn and now all attention is on you and him. You sense an altercation is coming. In the heat of the moment, you have forgotten to get off the train and it starts pulling away from the station. 'What is this farce?' you exclaim. you exclaim. You are now trapped with this rude man and a carriage full of spectators, having missed your stop and caused a scene. It's not hard to imagine this actually taking place. Every day we are faced with potential wrongdoings. People bang into us, take our seats and steal our popcorn (maybe I need to change my cinema).

The Stoics would approach this situation a little differently. When wronged by the rude man, they wouldn't allow it to affect them. Instead, they would whip out their stoic psychological strategies, such as reasoning, to overcome their negative emotions. The Stoic might reason that the world is made up of all types of people – happy, joyful, glum, disobedient, egotistical, arrogant, and rude – and today they met a rude one. That's it. It wasn't pleasant but they wouldn't let it distract them from the mission they were on, which was getting off the train.

Can you see how this approach is much more beneficial when it comes to making effective decisions? It's easy to give in to the emotion of frustration when someone insults you or wrongs you. It's much harder to focus on the fact that what has happened to you is an opportunity to reframe and test your stoic ability.

Another way that the Stoics would ensure they were able to be better at facing problematic times was to put themselves in difficulty. For example, this could be eating only rice and drinking water for a week (even though you can afford way more) or wearing the same clothes for a few days (even though you have a wardrobe decked out with all the latest threads). This exercise aims to still your mind by demonstrating that you can overcome hardships if they befall you. By testing your Stoicism every once in a while you will become more confident in your ability and panic less when tough times happen, as they inevitably will. To put this into context a little more, let me explain the four stoic virtues that Stoicism is built upon.

Stoic virtues

1. Wisdom – the ability to choose your response.
2. Courage – the ability to know your values, face situations head-on, do the right thing

even when others are rewarded for doing the quick, easy or wrong thing.

3. Temperance – the ability to maintain balance (they are neither excessive nor deprived), exercise self-control and understand that both pleasure and pain are fleeting.

4. Justice – the ability to care for others; we are all connected and want good for the whole.

The link between Stoic philosophy and decision-making is apparent if you look at the four virtues of Stoicism and then consider what it would mean to live your life by these principles.

For example, if you decided to test out the Stoic philosophy and challenged yourself to practise these four virtues daily in all situations, it is likely you would experience some radical changes that could include increasing your tolerance to pain, having a different interpretation of struggle, and learning to distinguish what is in your control and, crucially, what isn't. The practice would cause you to respond differently to the world and lead you to make different and, perhaps, better decisions.

Ultimately, as William B. Irvine, said, 'The pursuit of virtue results in a degree of tranquillity, which in turn makes it easier for us to pursue virtue.' And what you have there is a truly virtuous circle!

This affects not only decision-making, but also mental toughness, because a person with guiding principles in their life is likely to make better decisions than someone who is just taking life as it comes, based on feeling, independent judgement and past experience. It also extends the thinking behind being completely responsible for ourselves and our actions, learning to control what we can and accepting the things we can't, as well as turning challenges into advantages.

For example, getting fired from your job could either be seen as a complete disaster or an opportunity for rebirth, starting your own business and becoming more self-reliant. If someone entertains the latter rather than languishing in despair, the situation provides a lesson, new frontiers and, possibly, a new and more valuable revenue stream.

3 Steps to having a stoic mindset

1. **Pause before you respond:** in life, we tend to always respond, react and move in a state of emotion. This step is about putting the brakes on that. It doesn't mean you don't speak; it means that you take a brief moment to consider your response before you act from a place of emotion. This has its distinct advantages, especially during arguments, where the propensity to say things we don't mean and then respond in a state of emotion is heightened. For example, if a colleague calls you tardy, consider first of all if there is any merit to their statement. If you are late,

improve your timekeeping, don't just snap back. They say that the best response to insults is self-improvement.

2. **Practice acceptance:** this relates to wisdom, peace and learning to figure out what you can control and what you can't, and how you'll then respond given this information. For example, it is out of your control which questions will appear on an exam paper, but how hard you practise for the exam is within your control.

3. **Don't get even, be fair:** don't seek to punish someone who wrongs you, such as your boss making an example of you in front of the whole team, or sulk moodily in the corner all day, think about what's fair. Again, this is to do with how you respond to the world (you can start to see the theme here). Responding to this situation with retribution and revenge in your heart will only make matters worse, but by learning to respond by doing what is right, what is fair and holding the boss to account will remove the emotional conflict and burden from yourself. Can you see how trying to get one over on them only makes things worse for you in the long run? Deal with what's fair instead, and you will empower yourself to be free from the whims of emotion.

Summary

- By practising Stoicism, you learn how to respond wisely to negative emotions.

- When facing situations, learn to reframe your emotions, and nervousness becomes excitement.

- Pause before you react and do what's right, not what's easy.

CHAPTER 8

STAY CALM: CLEAR YOUR MIND TO MAKE GOOD DECISIONS

"You are the sky. Everything else – it's just the weather."

— Pema Chödrön

FINALLY, TO ROUND off this section of the book, I will end with a chapter on calmness. In it, I am going to share a couple of tools to help you clear your mind so that you can remain still and reach an appropriate state to make excellent decisions. They say, don't make decisions when you're sad, nor commitments when you're happy, and I happen to agree that is a pretty good rule of thumb to operate by.

Calm decisions are better decisions

Remaining calm is advantageous at the best of times. But even those of us who manage to keep quite calm get tested when things go wrong. The natural reaction is to get frustrated, angry and make bad decisions that compound all of the above. For example, you've just landed in a new city for a number of important business meetings, your phone keeps buzzing, you can't locate the train station ticket booth and the train is about to depart. In this instance, you're trying to get multiple important tasks completed quickly and effectively.

The easy response would be to get flustered, lose your composure and then take it out on the lowly train conductor who actually has the information you need but decides not to help you as much as he could because you've barked at him aggressively. This causes you to get lost again and miss the train. You are now late for every meeting and your phone's about to die due to all the ringing.

Consider now an alternative approach. You realise that time is of the essence and notice you're starting to get uncomfortable with all the things you need to do in a very short space of time. In kicks your inner guide that remembers this is the perfect moment to practise regaining your calmness. You take a moment to close your eyes and take five deep, long breaths. The exercise takes you less than 30 seconds to complete. As you open your eyes to the world again you notice a friendly-looking conductor standing by the turnstile to the train station. As you approach, you remind yourself to remain calm and clearly ask where you can get a ticket for the train. The ticket conductor decides to escort you to the ticket booth himself because you asked so very graciously and it is difficult to find. Moments later you have purchased a ticket and are boarding a carriage with a table and power bank to put your phone on charge whilst you respond to the messages. As you speed towards your destination, you feel proud of not letting your emotions control the outcome of the last 10 minutes and look forward to the meetings ahead.

Can you see how calmness is the key ingredient here to saving the day and not making the situation worse (even if this has never happened to you, you will know how it feels to have your travel plans messed up)? To try this out, I challenge you to respond with calmness the next time you feel frustrated, and see how much this improves the situation.

Imagine it's Monday morning and you're trying to send out a bunch of emails to prospects before the day gets underway because you know that they're more likely to read them at 8.30am on the commute, but there's a snag. Your computer keeps crashing and the little rainbow-coloured wheel is menacingly swirling, as if it's taunting you.

When this happens, see it as an opportunity to regain a sense of calm. There are times when you're better off slowing down or stepping away completely to regain the inner peace that leads to a high-quality decision-making process.

I realise it can be difficult to initiate this practice. It's natural if you want to keep taking action towards the course you've already set, and think, 'I must get those emails out regardless.' However, due to the rush, mistakes are made, typos are left unfixed and the overall professionalism of the emails is compromised. This pressure not to stop and take stock sabotages our mental state, leading us straight to a cascade of potentially disastrous decisions that further complicate and compound the issue.

If in doubt, get centred, take a walk for five minutes and regain your composure, it will pay dividends in the long run. Try it, you'll see.

But what if you've just got too much going on to become calm? If you've ever felt overwhelmed, you will know that it feels like your head just won't work. It happens to the best of us, right when we don't want it to, and how do we usually deal with it? By sticking our heads in the sand and pretending it's not a problem and carrying on regardless. I have come to realise that it is more important to recognise and acknowledge feelings such as a crowded mind, persistent dull headache and that pressured feeling that signals 'not enough time, too much to do'. It's almost as if we're walking on the precipice, tiptoeing along, and one little thing can throw us off balance, lose our train of thought and send our tightly held composure into a spin.

If this sounds like you, then I want to share a couple of tips with you that will remove you from the grip of emotional headwinds, as well as some steps to gain inner calm and move forward.

Steps to deal with overwhelm

Step 1: remember that your time is valuable. It's not always your job to say yes to every request, so learn to say no instead. As you become more successful in your career, you'll find that demands for your time will increase. The critical part here is to remember that you already have important commitments you have made to yourself, whether this is your family, friends or your health. If you're feeling overwhelmed on a regular basis, maybe it's time to shed a few extra *yeses* that you automatically committed to without consciously thinking about it that should have been *nos*. Highly successful individuals achieve the things they desire because they have the willpower and strength to say no to a lot of things. This might sound counter-intuitive, but the ability to say no to things, people and situations that don't support your vision leaves you free to really go for it and take advantage of the opportunities that do. Warren Buffet, Tim Ferriss and many others state that one of the main reasons for their success is they say no to almost everything. Now, I know what you're thinking, 'How do I know when to say "no"?' and 'What if I miss out on something that I later regret?' This bit is easy, you just need to learn to exercise your saying no muscle much more frequently. This is a valuable lesson that, if actioned, will see you do great things. It takes purpose and grit to stick to, but believe me, the rewards are there if you can make this simple but effective tweak to your automatic response process.

Step 2: before you agree to anything, ask yourself whether it is important to your vision. The key to focusing on what is actually important to you is to consistently ask yourself, does what you're about to spend an evening doing align with your values, vision and where you are headed? Ask this question every time a demand for your attention is made. By getting clear on this and assessing things based on these criteria rather than just responding willy-nilly, you can create space in your life for calmness.

The next time you are faced with a potential commitment, e.g. a friend invites you to dinner at a new restaurant opening in town, or you receive an invitation to a client's launch party, or it's one of the children's dad's birthdays from pre-school on Saturday afternoon, I want you to STOP and question whether this is taking you closer to your goals or adding more to your already overfull plate.

At first, it might seem strange, like you're turning down opportunities to network and connect with other people, but when you are overwhelmed, ambitious and know where you're headed, events and commitments attended out of guilt will only lead to further stress and, you guessed it, more overwhelm. By taking the advice of other super achievers and questioning the demands on your time, you put yourself in pole position to focus and prioritise what's of importance to you.

Top strategies for staying calm

Now that we've dealt with one of the most common and frustrating blockers to calmness, I want to give you some strategies to get into the ideal state faster.

1. Acceptance

One of the most effective tools for regaining control over your emotions and getting back to a calm place is to accept your emotions for what they are.

This is one of the wisest of all paths to follow. By learning to first accept your feelings for what they are, and then accept yourself for feeling them, you can move past current feelings and into your desired state. The first stage of acceptance is being open to receiving the new emotional state you wish to feel.

For example, you've just received a text from a client demanding that you call them right away. It's late at night and you have spent most of the day at their beck and call, dealing with their ongoing tedious requests, and gone above and beyond to provide all the information they needed. Now their message is the last straw, it's interrupted your flow and has got you in a full-on tizz. Its tone is harsh, abrupt, and downright rude, and it shows no element of remorse for interrupting the sanctuary of your evening or apology for requiring your immediate attention at this late hour. You're angry and ready to unleash all kinds of whoopass as it has disturbed you just as you've started to unwind from a very stressful day.

Know the feeling? You've been there? That's what you're facing. Instead of swearing at your phone and taking it out on your partner, or calling the client with a hot head and damaging the relationship you've worked so hard to maintain, imagine that you just recognise those feelings, accept them and just breathe… whooossaaaa. You would now be much calmer and better able to respond to the message. I know this sounds really easy on paper, but all it takes is a moment to choose a new direction. By introducing that moment to pause and recognise what you are feeling, it will allow you to reach a new level of mental toughness and make better decisions. With the help of a few deep breaths, you can reprogram yourself to choose how you want to respond to this event. Remember what we learnt about the Stoics; their wisdom is knowing how to respond to the world. How you respond *is* in your control and when this is mastered, it will make you a world-class decision-maker.

3 Steps to acceptance

1. Recognise and acknowledge your feelings. By doing this, you honour the feeling for what it is (e.g. frustration, anger, rage, exasperation, annoyance).

2. Take 3-5 long deep breaths (in through your nose, out through your mouth) and focus your mind solidly on the opportunity ahead of you. Be grateful for the opportunity to do this business, build these relationships and have this moment in time as it is.

3. Remember the sense of urgency. You have a responsibility to act with speed, you won't be here forever. By highlighting this sobering fact, it can actually get you to focus on what this really means to you, the bigger picture and on to the potential opportunity. This line of thinking is about switching to a solution-focused mindset and taking stock of the bigger picture rather than focusing on the detail. It can be helpful to remember that life can be taken at any moment because emotions like anger are fleeting and damaging if they are acted on. By refocusing on the bigger picture, you can operate from a position of strength.

Once your mind makes this switch, you'll start to ease up, your body will become less tense and thoughts inspired by creativity, fun and empowerment will return. I would encourage you now to think about how you'd like to feel and welcome those specific feelings in. Allow yourself to get closer to these warm, enriching and enlightened thoughts, feelings and ideas. Holding yourself in this space will give your mind a chance to focus on what is of greatest importance.

2. Gratitude

Gratitude is a magic remedy for remaining calm because, by its very nature, it is the pathway to greatness. By experiencing gratitude, we energise the world around us with a higher vibration and this, in turn, attracts more positive energy to us, which then becomes a virtuous circle.

By focusing on what's *right* with the situation, what you have to be thankful for, and the vast magnificence of the bigger picture, the intensity of the situation is diminished, and the more negative elements are pushed into perspective. Think of gratitude as an amplifier of goodwill to you and those around you. The more love, joy and passion you give out to the world, the more will come back to you. A grateful person is centred, more likely to spot the opportunity and rise to the challenge when called upon. Gratitude really is one of the most powerful tools in your toolkit.

To ensure a positive energy state is maintained, it is advantageous to have a 'go-to' memory, object, person or event that you are grateful for in your mind. The key is to pick something to focus on that you are infinitely grateful for, and then when you recall this, gratitude will replace any negative energy, transforming it into positive, uplifting and aligned thoughts. This frequency allows your composure and perspective to return, so you can go forward with regained calm.

3. Know your triggers and create moments for calm

Of course, getting cool, calm and collected isn't always as easy as the self-help books make out (at first), but we can practise noticing our triggers and emotions until this becomes a habit. Let's face it, the world is full of noise, and I am not just talking about honking horns, Dolby Atmos surround sound or your CEO going through the latest company update over Google Hangouts. We are constantly bombarded with requests for our attention, on the Internet, on our phones and on the street. There's a call to action every which way you look and unless you live on a remote island in the Outer Hebrides (and I'm pretty sure even they have Tinder) you need to be aware of all these demands so that you can prioritise them.

What we allow ourselves to pay attention to matters. In the section below, I am going to spell out the conscious and subconscious influences on our decisions.

First off, broadly speaking, two types of triggers govern how we respond to the world around us. These are internal and external triggers. Internal triggers are generated by you, external ones by someone or something else. The point here is to create time for yourself to be alone and then be still with your thoughts. By understanding all the different pressures and triggers that you allow to take that most precious resource (your attention), you can guard it in the manner it deserves. It's like tipping all your money out on the street and expecting not to lose any. The same goes for your mental state, without creating the proper time for calm, the world will keep on draining and triggering you. The way to make better decisions is from a place of calm. Philosophers have known this for centuries, and in a world of increasing demands, the ability to still your mind has never been more relevant. Below are a few examples of common triggers, both internal and external.

Examples of internal triggers

- When you're sleepy, your eyes start to close, and you yawn.

- When your stomach makes a gurgling sound in the middle of the quiet part of an all-hands company meeting, you're hungry... (or experiencing painful bloating, in which case, I would recommend going to a pharmacy).

- When you are anxious, you feel a ball knotted up in your stomach, so you call a friend for reassurance.

- When you see your partner after a week away on a work trip, you feel joyous excitement inside.

Examples of external triggers

- When you get tagged in an Instagram story by that hot guy from the gym and your phone beeps with glee to notify you.

- When you get cornered at a networking event talking to a person you can bet your life on you'll never see again but they just won't stop talking and talking, it's as if you're long-lost best friends.

- When the microwave dings to let you know your spag bol is ready to eat.

- When a knock at the door alerts you to the fact someone's waiting outside.

- When your Amazon Alexa pipes up to remind you that it's your cousin's birthday and you really should buy them a gift (from Amazon).

These are all prompts that lead to behavioural change. By being aware of just how many demands for your attention there are, you can begin to manage them more closely and, better still, shut them off. For instance, turning off notifications when you are making important decisions or creating time for focused thought might be a strategy that will help you to make better overall decisions, or allocating 20 minutes a day for meditation could be another method.

Now I want to dive deeper into the psychology of persuasion and influence because you need to know how creative the world has really become before you can become a Jedi master of learning what to avoid and what to prioritise.

Marketers spend their days strategising how to get you to purchase by highlighting, prodding, poking and generally trying to make you feel bad that you don't have said product in your life.

That's how it used to work anyway. First, you stated the problem, then you proceeded to annoy the person and finally you presented the solution. This was an all too common method of influencing a customer to buy.

However, with all the complexity and noise out there, the game has changed. Consumers have become habituated to this old type of funnel. We've evolved and marketing has gotten smarter, with interlaced psychological triggers to get you to act without even knowing it. Author of *The New York Times* bestselling book, *Launch,* has spent a career coaching some of the most successful entrepreneurs in the online business world. His Product Launch Formula has taken the world by storm and transformed how products are sold online. Below is just a brief outline of how it works. I share this with you to demonstrate how impressively strategic the world has gotten in trying to take your most valuable resource from you. This is supposed to make you want to guard it more carefully. You also need to be more aware of the influences and tactics that are used to get us to behave in a certain way by subtly influencing our decision-making process.

Jeff Walker Product Launch Formula – 6 Mental Triggers

Jeff tells us that there are 6 mental triggers[5] that influence how we make decisions. These are:

- **Authority** – we pay more attention to authority figures, e.g. a doctor wearing a white coat

- **Community** – we act in accordance with the norms. Keeping up with the Joneses, e.g. if everyone else in the neighbourhood drives a Benz, then, guess what, we too will have a luxury car

- **Anticipation** – we look forward to events, e.g. weddings

- **Reciprocity** – if someone gives us something, you want to give back, e.g. sign up to their event if they came to yours

- **Social Proof** – if we see others doing something then we are inclined to do it ourselves, e.g. leaving a review/comment on Facebook

- **Scarcity** – if there is less of something, then we are super interested, e.g. a Lamborghini

When you think about the 6 mental triggers listed above, it is easy to see how our decision-making process can be hijacked by deeply imbedded influences. Sometimes, we might not even be sure why we feel strongly in a direction, but we know

---

[5] https://jeffwalker.com/

we need those comfy Ugg boots and the latest Gucci handbag or that shiny gold Rolex watch.

The crazy thing is that marketing experts know these 6 mental triggers and carefully structure their advertising campaigns to stimulate your desire to purchase more frequently, sign up, hit like, take part and act as a loyal advocate. All the while you are taking action in a certain way to hit their business objectives. Therefore, you must make it your mission to create pockets of time throughout the day when you can become calm and let yourself explore what is necessary instead of operating from a place of reaction.

In today's always-on, connected, attention-seeking environment, it's no wonder that we need to boost our mental toughness so that we do not get distracted and can actually get the most important things done. This is achieved by becoming calmer, not busier.

The way to become calmer is simple on paper, but harder to achieve in reality. However, there is a wealth of information out there right now, as this is a hugely important topic that we – humanity as a whole – are just realising the significance of. Philosophers, going back to the times of Marcus Aurelius and Seneca two thousand years ago, have always understood the goal of tranquillity and centring oneself, and I would say that we are only now seeing a resurgence of that come into the mainstream as it gains more popularity among the masses. I recommend reading *Stillness Is The Key* by Ryan Holiday and *Super Attractor* by Gabrielle Bernstein as two recent publications that draw on principles that are grounded in gaining both calmness and a deep sense of confidence to let go.

If you're not a reader, which would be strange as you've got this far in the book, there are Apps like *Calm*, *Headspace* and *Idillionaire* available online that can help to create daily breaks to find stillness in your day. If you struggle to find that sense of peace in everyday life, download them right now. Take advantage of the free trial and make the decision today to allow yourself the gift of making good decisions by being calmer. Millions of people would do better at work, have more loving relationships, and gain just about everything they wanted if they could slow down for a second and regain control of their emotions without chasing the frayed edges of their existence in search of pleasure or the avoidance of pain. If we could just be still and comfortable with our own thoughts, I believe we would get closer to a flow state and, as a result, our decision-making would be infinitely improved.

To give you some encouragement from the entrepreneurial billionaire world, Bill Gates takes a week off every year and goes to his cabin in the woods. He calls this Think Week. Bill Gates! Can you imagine, the second richest person in the world (currently at $106.2b) takes a week out of his hectic schedule each year to go by himself to a cabin just to think.

And he's not the only one. Marc Benioff, founder of Salesforce, who is also a billionaire, takes two weeks off every year to unplug from technology. That's right! Unplug! Benioff, founder of one of the largest tech giants in the world, takes himself to Hawaii to soak up the atmosphere and mull over ideas on where to take the company next. In a recent trip, he came back with a 'divide and conquer' strategy which saw him appoint a joint CEO so that he could focus his efforts on things that he enjoys, like philanthropy. Shares of Salesforce went up 34% in 2018 at a time when the wider market experienced contraction. If he's not doing something right, I don't know what right looks like.

> **There is a theme here – having the time to make good decisions and focus your energy on work that matters is something we all need to make time for, no matter how busy we are.**

The pursuit of this state of being is highly sought after, and if 'unplugging', 'think weeks' and making decisions to go in a new direction and regain our most valuable resource of time is where the nirvana is at, then it is clearly something we should all consider.

Summary

To round off this section on regaining calm and making it a priority, we've spoken about acceptance, the importance of expressing gratitude and the triggers that try to pull us in different directions on a daily basis.

Just by understanding that these mechanics are at play, you have taken one step closer to increasing your ability to regain calm in your life. My final tip is not to be too hard on yourself. The next time you are facing an important decision, take a step back, work through all the potential distractions, notice them and forgive yourself. Once you get into the habit of choosing how you respond to the environment around you, the ball is firmly placed back in your court. The more frequently you are able to acknowledge and reroute towards your desired outcome by taking actions to get calm, still and centred, the better you will ultimately become at it. What we focus on expands, and the principle works the same in this valuable arena.

FINAL REMARKS

I TRULY HOPE this book has been helpful to you and that sharing the lessons I learned whilst facing the toughest challenge I have ever (rightly or wrongly) had the (good/bad) fortune to face, has given you a new way to go about things and some new tools to work with.

It's an interesting world that we find ourselves in and the art of making high-quality decisions is crucial. With more competing demands for our time than ever before, it's imperative that we learn to adapt and skill up in this area to take full advantage of the opportunities that lie ahead.

I hope this book has given you advice on how to go about making decisions when it really matters. There are times that we must make choices, sometimes uncomfortable ones, but if we can learn to open our minds up to the possibility of the world, implement the strategies at our fingertips and make a commitment to always learn, we'll get some pretty effective outcomes.

Go forth and live the life of your biggest dreams. You are a force to be reckoned with and we are all only one decision away from the next chapter.

It has been an absolute pleasure and an honour serving you in this way, and if my story helped you at all I would really appreciate it if you could please post a review on social platforms, like Amazon, Goodreads, Facebook, to help spread this important message. Or pass this book on to a friend or family member who has some big decisions coming up. The better we all get at this, the more opportunity we each have to achieve our fullest potential and collectively make better decisions on a global scale. Remember, you are only one decision away from a totally different life.

With much gratitude,
Tim

ACKNOWLEDGEMENTS

I FEEL ABSOLUTELY humbled and blessed to have such wonderfully amazing friends and family in my life. It is only through their support, encouragement and love that these books get created and I have the platform to tell my story.

To my loving wife Sandra, without you by my side, the world would not spin as magically, and the sun would not shine so brightly. Thank you for actively pushing me, for being there and coming on this journey we are creating together. I love you.

I would like to make a special mention to my Auntie Judy, who along with many others in my family has helped support me since the passing of my mother. Her energy, high spirits and enthusiasm have kept me going in some of my darkest moments and helped me celebrate in my times of joy. People like Auntie Judy should be recognised for the positivity that they inspire in others, and if it were not for her carrying on after my mum, I am not sure where I would be. Auntie Judy is a courageous, passionate, and beautiful woman who welcomes you with open arms. Thank you for being you, and for being an inspiration to me and many others.

In the same vein, my mum has lit a fire in me that has, I am sure, led to my motto being 'believe it is possible'. Thank you for teaching me to go for it,

Mum, for believing in me fully and for showing me how to own and express my truth. Going on that trip with you to Verbier and having the honour of knowing someone as remarkable as you has given me so much. The world's abundance has been flowing because you helped me to dream big and believe in a vision greater than myself.

To Leila Green and the Known Publishing team, it is always such a pleasure working with you. You have become like a little London family that I pick up the phone to and then work intensely with over the months and years it takes to craft my work. The book writing process with you guys is second to none, and I am just so grateful to have you with me every time we do this. You push me to ask more from myself and the deep level of consideration, sheer effort and care you take working on my books is always astounding and thrilling at the same time. You set the bar high and go above and beyond to produce outstanding work. It never ceases to amaze me.

To you, the reader, thank you for picking up this book and reading my story about my near-death experience. You rock! This experience changed my perspective on life. I wanted to share it with you because it is my hope that by writing it down and exploring the lessons I learned, you can all see that with faith, a vision and some critical decision-making, we can scale the cliff face and live to tell the tale.

We are all on our own journey and each of us has our precipice to conquer. Just know that you are not alone. We can do it together by collectively figuring out the way when we share our own experiences.

ABOUT THE AUTHOR

Tim Castle is an author, success coach and speaker. His motto for life is 'believe it is possible'. Tim lives by this philosophy day in, day out, and has achieved a number of accolades, including multiple moves to new continents, completing extreme travel expeditions, an MBA and heading up sales and business development across Asia Pacific for a number of innovative technology companies.

He currently lives in Singapore with his wife and baby son and is loving every minute of it.

10% of profits from this book will go towards helping destitute children in Asia.

www.timjscastle.com

 @TimJSCastle

 @TimJSCastle

 @TimJSCastle

REFERENCES

https://hbr.org/2015/11/3-timeless-rules-for-making-tough-decisions

https://www.ted.com/talks/ray_dalio_how_to_build_a_company_where_the_best_ideas_win?language=en

https://hbr.org/2016/03/a-checklist-for-making-faster-better-decisions

https://hbr.org/2009/11/make-better-decisions-2

https://www.toolshero.com/decision-making/six-thinking-hats-de-bono/

http://proffittmanagement.com/thinking-styles-what-color-is-your-hat/

https://www.mindtools.com/pages/article/avoiding-psychological-bias.htm

https://www.mindtools.com/pages/article/newTED_07.htm

https://jeffwalker.com/

ALSO BY THE AUTHOR

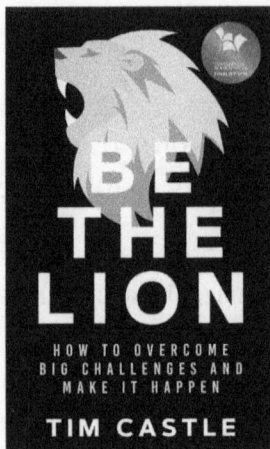

Want to achieve more without the stress and overwhelm?

As an ambitious person, I inevitably have a lot on my plate. In just two years, I went through pretty much every life change you can imagine. I planned our wedding, got married, moved jobs, moved countries, wrote and published a book, completed an MBA, became a father to my baby son, and then coped with his sudden serious illness, all whilst working full time.

I had to be the lion. I created new habits and thought patterns, and reconnected with my purpose to get sh*t done. I became stronger, a master of time management, productivity, and motivation. As a result my goals got closer. And there was a surprising side-effect: I became happier and more relaxed.

Let me show you how to set the bar high and succeed.

I distilled everything I learned into my 4Cs model, which enables you to overcome any challenge. This book explains the 4Cs and teaches processes, strategies, and optimisations to turbocharge your life. This system will help you to achieve more, without any of the stress, overwhelm, and fear that often comes with big life changes. Taking yourself to the next level and achieving huge success should be joyful. So let's have some fun....

THE ART OF
NEGOTIATION

**HOW TO GET
WHAT YOU WANT
(EVERY TIME)**

TIM CASTLE

Anyone can learn to become a good negotiator. Let me show you how.

I became a professional negotiator at the age of 23, and within just 12 months, I was single-handedly negotiating $1,000,000 deals. Being a negotiator has been such an empowering experience, and I've been able to transfer my professional skills into my personal life. Whether it's buying a home, budgeting for a wedding, or even buying a car, we all need to negotiate. In this book, I'll share insider tips, as well as teach you how to master the fundamentals, set clear objectives, overcome obstacles (i.e. turn 'no' into 'yes') and build long-term relationships, whether you are negotiating for yourself, or on behalf of your business. I will also give you practical advice and run through real-world scenarios to ensure you have the confidence to tackle your next negotiation head on. Ready to see what you can achieve?